My Holy War

My Holy War

Dispatches from the Home Front

Jonathan Raban

NEW YORK REVIEW BOOKS

nyrb

New York

THIS IS A NEW YORK REVIEW BOOK

PUBLISHED BY THE NEW YORK REVIEW OF BOOKS

MY HOLY WAR
by Jonathan Raban

Copyright © 2006 by Jonathan Raban

Copyright © 2006 by NYREV, Inc.

All rights reserved.

This edition published in 2006
in the United States of America by
The New York Review of Books
1755 Broadway
New York, NY 10019
www.nybooks.com

Library of Congress Cataloging-in-Publication Data

Raban, Jonathan.
    My holy war : dispatches from the home front / Jonathan Raban.
        p. cm. — (New York Review Books collection)
    ISBN 1-59017-175-6 (cloth)
    1. United States — Politics and government — 2001–. 2. United States
— Social conditions — 1980–. 3. September 11 Terrorist Attacks, 2001
— Influence. 4. War on Terrorism, 2001– — Political aspects — United States.
    5. War on Terrorism, 2001– — Social Aspects — United States.
    6. Iraq War, 2003. 7. Political culture — United States. 8. United States
—Description and travel. 9. Raban, Jonathan — Travel — United States.
I. Title. II. Series.
E902.R33 2005
973.931 — dc22
                                                                    2005022655

ISBN-13: 978-1-59017-123-3
ISBN-10: 1-59017-123-3
Printed in the United States of America on acid-free paper.
1 3 5 7 9 10 8 6 4 2

For Barbara Cairns, in whose house and garden many of these pieces began life in conversation.

Contents

I

Introduction

PIETY & IRON

ON SEPTEMBER 11, 2001, the United States reflexively contracted around the wound inflicted on its eastern seaboard, and for a short spell the country felt as small as Switzerland. Twenty-eight hundred miles west of the World Trade Center, roused by the phone ringing at 5:55 AM, I switched on the TV in time to see the second jetliner, flying at a tilt, aimed at the south tower like a barbed harpoon arrowing through the blue. It seemed at that moment as if the entire city around me were holding its breath. The bedroom window was open, but the usual white noise of a weekday waking morning was eerily absent. Somehow, in the eighteen minutes since the first strike on the north tower, everybody knew, and everybody was watching CNN. Unlike any news I can remember, news of September 11 was almost exactly simultaneous with the events themselves.

The blatant symbolism of the attacks—transcontinental American passenger jets destroying American skyscrapers—left no room for doubt as to their intended target. If you happened to live in Seattle, or Portland, or San Francisco, you were not excluded: the plane-bombs were squarely directed at the great abstraction of "America," its economic daily life, its government, its military power; and every resident of the United States had reason to feel that he or she was under assault by the terrorists. September 11 was unique in this: other shocking and violent events in the American past were relatively specialized and local—the assassinations of presidents, the destruction of a naval fleet, the mass murder of children at a school, the fiery annihilation of an eccentric cult, the blowing up of a federal building. Except when they occurred in your neighborhood or line of work, they were about other people. September 11 was different because it was so clearly and insistently about us. Although only some three thousand people actually died, out of a population of nearly three hundred million, everyone living in America that morning could feel that we were, in some more than merely metaphoric sense, survivors.

An unnatural quiet pervaded the city. Emptied of civilian aircraft, the sky was silent except for the rare snarl of a low-flying fighter jet. On Interstate 5, which bisects Seattle, the thin traffic moved at the solemn pace of a cortege, everyone keeping his distance, no one leaning on the horn, no one breaking ranks to get ahead. The sense of awful occasion was reinforced by the withdrawal of commercials from the networks: the sudden banishment of shrilling upbeat salesmen lent to the day the air of a Presbyterian sabbath. In the neighborhoods, strangers were talking to strangers on the street. It was much as older Londoners fondly describe the Blitz—a time when people discovered in themselves an unexpected capacity to behave as members of a warm and supportive community, huddling together in the face of a common enemy. This was the gift momentarily bestowed on us by the attacks, though it would not be long before the gift revealed itself to be a Trojan horse.

But in the days immediately following September 11, America felt strangely snug and comradely, protected by its military aircraft and the red-and-white-liveried Coast Guard gunboats on Puget Sound. The President then was a relatively minor character, overshadowed by the ubiquitous figure of Rudolph Giuliani, who brought to Ground Zero qualities that he had previously kept well hidden—candor, modesty, and, most striking of all, a bleak wit delivered with perfect timing. When Giuliani, skin stretched taut over a face drained of color, pushed back his Yankees cap to say, with a twisted grin, to prospective visitors to New York City, "You might actually have a better chance of getting tickets to *The Producers* now," he established himself as mayor of the nation. America needed Giuliani's barely inflected, rusty-hinge plainspeaking far more than it did George W. Bush's poorly rehearsed ghostwritten eloquence.

That week, my compatriot Christopher Hitchens, stranded in Seattle after giving a lecture in Walla Walla, Washington, on September 10, said over dinner that "at times like this, America turns into a one-party state," and reminded me of the prophecy made by Robert Lowell back in 1966, when he answered a questionnaire sent to him by the editors of *Partisan Review*:

> I have a gloomy premonition . . . that we will soon look back on this troubled moment as a golden time of freedom and license to act and speculate. One feels the sinews of the tiger, an ascetic, "moral" and authoritarian reign of piety and iron.

The mood of our fellow diners in the restaurant was one of forced joviality—a few jokes and laughs too many were coming from the tables around us. "I think we've just entered the reign of piety and iron," Hitchens said.

The remark rang in my head the next day, Saturday, when I drove out of Seattle with my eight-year-old daughter, on the flimsy excuse that we needed to buy eggs from a small farm in the Snoqualmie valley. I wanted to see how rural dwellers were responding to the attacks, and we were barely out of the city when the improvised roadside shrines began, with their prayer cards, two-stick crucifixes, wilting balloons, and pendulous stalactites of colored candle wax. In the valley, it seemed that every house was flying Old Glory. The flags fluttered from windows, fence posts, clotheslines (Wal-Mart reported the sales of 500,000 American flags in the days immediately following September 11.) One householder in the town of Carnation had stapled together three bedsheets to accommodate the message, painted in massive irregular black letters, GOD HElP BLeSS AMERiCA. We were out of luck on the eggs front: earlier in the week, a wandering gang of coyotes had slaughtered all the hens. In the light of this murderous attack, the farmer and his wife were understandably the only people I met that day for whom the events of Tuesday morning appeared to be remote, though their sadness and anger amply rivaled those of their neighbors, and the farmer's phrase "mindless killing!" was perfectly in tune with the national feeling of the moment.

That trip to the Snoqualmie valley was on my mind when, on July 7, 2005, the day of the Tube bombings that killed fifty-two people, I drove out of London, again with my daughter in tow. We left the city at 3 PM (the bombs had gone off at 8:50 AM) and fed ourselves into the agonizingly slow-moving swarm of traffic on the South Circular Road. Five hours later, after a couple of brief stops, we reached the village of Aynho in Northamptonshire, less than seventy miles from London. At the pub-hotel where we found a room for the night, I took my notebook into the bar, expecting that the bombings would dominate the conversation there. Oddly, the air rang with the names of racing drivers—Schumacher, Montoya, Villeneuve, Coulthard. It took a few moments for the penny to drop: we were just fifteen miles from Silverstone, Britain's main Formula One racetrack, on the eve of the qualifying races for Sunday's grand prix. There was no communal sense of shock, or grief, or great occasion; only a steady rumble of complaint that the enormous traffic jams following the bombings had delayed the arrival at the pub of numerous friends and family members (and providentially freed our room as the result of a last-minute cancellation).

For the next ten days, our travels took us all over England, north and south, and it was astonishing to find how little the coordinated attacks appeared to have impinged on people's thoughts and lives. I was the bomb-bore, nearly always the first to raise the subject, which elicited mostly only weary recognition and memories of the IRA bombs and bomb scares in the 1970s and early 1980s. Although the news media were labeling the events "7/7" and giving them vast and dramatic space, the pub-crawling visitor would have found it hard to detect from the buzz of talk that anything of exceptional significance had recently happened in England.

It was only on July 21, when the second, failed attack took place, and we were back in London, that the mood changed and the country appeared to be genuinely rattled. But even then there was no American-style talk of "war": these were unambiguously criminal acts, to be handled by the police; and when a Brazilian electrician with no connection to the bombings, Jean Charles de Menezes, who was living in England on an expired visa, was shot to death by police officers at Stockwell Tube station in south London on July 22, the event caused outrage comparable to that aroused by the two sets of bombings themselves.

Initially, the Blair government responded to the attacks with exemplary coolness, determinedly refusing to go along with the Bush administration's extravagant and bellicose rhetoric on the danger posed by radical Islamism. But tabloid papers like the *Sun* and the *Daily Mail*, known in the UK as the "red-tops," mounted an onslaught against Blair, accusing him of being soft on terrorism, failing to prevent terrorists settling in Britain under the guise of "asylum-seekers," and allowing the capital city to turn into "Londonistan." In August, just before he departed on a family holiday at a secret location, Blair announced a raft of ill-thought-out "anti-terror" measures, which precipitated a fierce exchange of fire between the government and the judiciary. Having shown commendable bravery and restraint in the face of the bombers, Blair, or so it seemed at the time, had quailed before the force majeure of the tabloid press.

* * *

In 2001 piety and iron came hand in hand, but piety led the way. The roadside shrines and public prayers were part of a great outpouring of uninhibited religiosity that would have been unthinkable in a European country. On September 11 George W. Bush quoted the 23rd Psalm, and spoke of the conflict (though not yet the war) between "good and evil." A Harlem gospel choir sang hymns in the ruins of the World Trade Center. Members of the US Congress sang "God Bless America," on the steps of the Capitol, and a month later passed a resolution to encourage both the use of the slogan and the singing of Irving Berlin's song in public schools. On September 16, Bush announced that America was now embarked on a "crusade":

> This is a new kind of evil, and we understand, and the American people are now beginning to understand, this crusade, this war on terrorism, is going to take a while....

At the time I heard it said that Bush used the word by accident and was probably ignorant of its significance, which seems unlikely, given the amount of writing and rewriting that goes into presidential speeches. Perhaps Bush himself was not entirely aware of what he was saying, but some White House scribe surely intended to put us at least loosely in mind of Richard Coeur de Lion...

> Richard, that robbed the lion of his heart
> And fought the holy wars in Palestine.
> —Shakespeare, *King John*

Certainly the authors of the phrase "Operation Infinite Justice" (later amended to "Operation Enduring Freedom"), used to describe the mobilization of the American military for the invasion of Afghanistan, must have known that infinite justice is an attribute of the

Almighty in both fundamentalist Christian and Muslim theology. After September 11, America meant to play God in the world—not gentle Jesus but wrathful, thunderous Jehovah.

It took a few days before the iron of war came clearly into view. To begin with, it appeared to be a toss-up as to whether the attacks were an act of warfare against the US or a "crime against humanity" whose perpetrators should be apprehended then tried and sentenced in the courts. Bush's first uses of the word "war" sounded more figurative than actual, as if he were talking about a war on poverty or drugs, and it wasn't until September 20, when he addressed the joint session of Congress, that he unveiled the ambitious dimensions of a new hot war, to be fought on a global scale against an enemy that "by abandoning every value except the will to power" was the true descendant of "fascism, and Nazism, and totalitarianism." On the home front, he announced the appointment of Tom Ridge as the head of the newly created umbrella department of Homeland Security; to the troops, he said, "The hour is coming when America will act, and you will make us proud." Once again he stressed the religious component of the conflict, in a form of words that suggested a good deal of to-ing and fro-ing on the part of officials and speechwriters made nervous by the earlier use of "crusade": "Freedom and fear, justice and cruelty, have always been at war, and we know that God is not neutral between them."

Even as Bush was speaking in Washington, D.C., the rest of the country was just beginning to unclench from the extraordinary sense of bipartisan solidarity and closeness of the week and a half before. The physical distance between the two urban coasts had started to reassert itself, and by sometime in October it seemed that Seattle had actually grown further away from the East Coast than it had been before September 11. No amount of TV and newspaper coverage could keep the affront of the attacks alive for us in the way it was alive for residents of New York, D.C., and Pennsylvania: we couldn't taste the reek of dust from Ground Zero in our throats, or be daily reminded of the gross mutilation of our own skyline. In coast-to-coast phone conversations, we'd hear that our interlocutor's neighbor, cousin, or friend of a friend had died on September 11, but such reports tended only to further underline our remoteness from the events, the strong muffling effect of America's enormous geography.

Another kind of distance was also in play. Other Democrat-voting cities were still coming gingerly to terms with the new presidential administration, but Seattle's mind had been made up long before September 11: for reasons peculiar to the region, it detested the Bush White House. Politics in the Pacific Northwest devolve less on social than on environmental issues: land use, forests, salmon, wilderness preservation. Seattle liberals are animals of a different stripe from their counterparts in other cities—markedly illiberal in their zeal, their steely, take-no-prisoners fervor on matters like climate change, the Kyoto accords, nuclear power, logging in national forests, the Endangered Species Act, oil drilling in the Arctic National Wildlife Refuge (it's an ancient Seattle conceit that all of Alaska is in the city's personal backyard). The Bush administration, packed with energy industry executives, was, from the moment of its election in 2000, the declared enemy of everything dear to Seattle's liberal heart.

So the impulse to rally around the presidency in the wake of September 11 was weaker here than elsewhere, even on the urban West Coast, which was generally far more lukewarm than the eastern seaboard. Blanket mistrust of Bush administration motives and intentions extended automatically from its energy policies to its "war on terror" and its invasions of Afghanistan and Iraq. Provincial isolation from the attacks played some part, but the deep and angry ideological rift between the city and the administration was at least equally important in shaping Seattle's reluctance to sign up for Bush's wars.

It's tempting to remember the last days of September and the first days of October 2001, when Operation Enduring Freedom was taking rapid shape, as a time of broad national consensus, but it did not feel like that here, where people still clung to the notion that the proper way of dealing with Osama bin Laden was for the world's police forces to combine, winkle him out of his hiding place, and put him on trial at the International Court of Justice in The Hague. The brutal igneous geography of Afghanistan, which had defeated the Soviets in the 1980s and the British a hundred years before, would lead American forces into a "quagmire," code word for Vietnam, though curiously inappropriate for Afghanistan's rocky and generally unboggy terrain. Pacifist voices—louder and more numerous here than on the East Coast—argued that the answer to violence was not escalation of violence. One aspect of the coming invasion that did gain wide support on this coast was the feminist case for liberating women from their iniquitous repression by Mullah Omar and the Taliban. But a review of editorials and readers' letters published in Seattle's two daily papers, the *Times* and the *Post-Intelligencer*, between September 25 and October 8 (the day after the bombing began) shows a city deeply skeptical of the need for military as opposed to legal action, and congenitally suspicious of the true intent of the administration as it led the country to war against the Taliban.

Within hours of the first rain of cruise missiles on Taliban positions, the *Post-Intelligencer* ran an editorial darkly titled "This Will Be a Very Long War," in which it acknowledged that a military response to the "vile crime committed on American soil" was "justifiable." The assault on Afghanistan was "one salvo in a war that may take years to win, if it can be won at all," and the uncertainty raised in that phrase suffused the piece. "But we lose the moral high ground if our pursuit of justice is conducted unjustly," wrote the editorialists, raising the powerful suspicion that such unjust conduct might be more likely than otherwise: "The failure to be true to our own moral values will give lie to our vision of justice"—a sentence that now reads like simple clairvoyance, in the light of Bagram, Abu Ghraib, and Guantánamo Bay.

We trust that the order to begin was preceded by elaborate caution and extensive intelligence. And when it's over we expect a full explanation of the mission's justification and intent and an accurate accounting of its results.

The words "trust" and "expect" carry with them such a strong whiff of "mistrust" and "doubt" that this queasy endorsement of the President ranks alongside Mark Antony's endorsement of Brutus.

If the city was dubious and unhappy about the invasion of Afghanistan, it saw no merit whatever in the invasion of Iraq. The local press, and local politicians such as Congressman Jim McDermott and Senator Patty Murray, were among the first in the country to label the supposed connection between the Saddam regime and al-Qaeda as an opportunist fiction. On weapons of mass destruction, Seattle was more inclined to listen sympathetically to Hans Blix than to the President. As for the rhetorically high-minded part of the enterprise—the liberation of the oppressed people of Iraq—it may be that Seattle, a city cram-full of philanthropic nonprofits, many of them devoted to supplying food and medical aid to the developing world, found it harder than most to accept the idea that tanks, bombs, and missiles were likely to improve the lot of the unfortunates for whom rich Seattle, with its endless round of lakeside social fund-raisers, had a corporate tender heart. At any rate, from summer's end in 2002, the NO IRAQ WAR signs began to sprout so thickly that in my own neighborhood the absence of a sign looked like a mark of political eccentricity.

Stricken New York—another liberal city—offered a very different kind of liberal discourse, and nowhere more strikingly than in the pages of *The New Yorker*, whose editor, David Remnick, and chief political commentator, Hendrick Hertzberg, wrote, sometimes individually and sometimes in tandem, a long series of front-of-the-book pieces on the Bush administration's evolving responses to September 11 and its translation of the war on terror into the war on Iraq. The magazine's offices on Times Square were just four miles from the wreckage of the twin towers, and *The New Yorker*'s intimate proximity to the events deeply colored its editorial coverage. Remnick's and Hertzberg's pieces were cautious, full of caveats, nuanced to a fault: they were shot through with New York's grief and New York's anger, but strove for a tone of judicious restraint and detachment even as they gave full weight to the emotions of those closest to the scene of the attacks. They read like an exercise in anguished tightrope walking as they balanced liberal distaste for the "arrogance" and "bullyboy unilateralism" of the Bush administration's public face with a sort of grim recognition that, on the whole, excepting this, excepting that, the administration was broadly on the right track in its prosecution of the war on terrorism in which Iraq emerged, in Bush's words, as "the central front."

It was uncomfortable to read these pieces in Seattle. One might be—I was—unpersuaded by their chicken-hawk conclusions, but the painfully qualified terms in which they were phrased made the conversation to be heard in my corner of the US seem callow in its unwavering certitude. It struck me then that on the East Coast everyone must be staying up late into the night, wrangling over dinner tables about the rights and wrongs of liberal interventionism, while where I lived, anyone who suggested that there might be a "right" in it would be quickly shouted down—at least on the western side of Lake Washington.

Always the vantage point critically alters the character of the view. Seattle habitually looks westward to Asia and has its back turned to Washington, D. C., "the other Washington," as people like to call it here—a distant, generally tiresome city, given to much unnecessary interference in Seattle's international trading activities. When Seattle looks at the war on terror, the Patriot Act, the Bush administration's foreign policy, it's more likely to hold up a mirror to its own face than to focus a telescope on the eastern horizon.

The threat of terrorism is a matter of anxious concern here: Seattle's docks, crowded with ships from China, Japan, South Korea, and the Philippines, are separated from its business district only by a somewhat rickety highway viaduct, erected in 1953 and weakened by intermittent earthquake damage. Seattle also fears what might come from the sky, for it is uneasily conscious that it's the nearest metropolitan city in the US to Pyongyang, and thoughts of North Korea's nuclear capabilities are more prone to disturb Seattle's sleep than that of cities on the Atlantic coast.

When John Ashcroft's Justice Department targeted Arab visitors and immigrants for "registration," the move awakened in Seattle a guilty memory of its participation in the 1942 internment of several thousands of its own Japanese-American citizens (they were first transported to a kind of temporary Guantánamo Bay in the southern suburbs of the city, named Camp Harmony by the US Army). More than most cities, Seattle has reason to quail at the prospect of America going on a witch hunt for strangers in its midst, and its deep aversion to the Patriot Act ("It's become a patriotic act to oppose the Patriot Act," wrote the editorial board of the *Post-Intelligencer* in the summer of 2003) has complex roots, of which reflexive liberal principle is only one. A thick streak of far-western libertarianism is an essential part of Seattle's character. So is an almost fanatical regard for privacy in this sprawling, low-rise city where, seen from the air, every house appears to shun its neighbor from behind a dense shelter-belt of inky shrubs and evergreens. Ashcroft's enthusiastic (and notably Calvinistic) vision of a surveillance society, with mailmen and meter readers reporting back on the lives of private citizens, no sin-concealing drapes in windows, every soul open to the gaze of government as if to God, was much like Cotton Mather's dream of a reformed New England, but it went down very badly indeed in Seattle.

Through 2002 and 2003, Seattle fell further and further out of step with the Bush administration and its responses, foreign and domestic, to September 11. At the same time it was also increasingly alienating itself from its own relatively conservative rural and suburban hinterland. I sometimes felt as if I were living on an offshore island, looking across a mysteriously widening strait to a mainland coast that was fast turning mauve in the distance. Some of that sense of insular detachment shows up in the pieces that follow here.

Not long after September 11, my phone began to ring. Because I'd once written a book about Arabia, and had since written several about—or set in—the United States, a handful of editors with good memories in both London and New York thought I might have something to say about the present situation. The London ones had the notion that I could explain, or at least try to describe, something of the mood of America on its vengeful warpath; the New York ones suggested that I might have picked up on my travels some clue to the motives of Islamist terrorists and their war on America. With a novel stalled in midstream (like every other novel that was being written in September 2001), I jumped at the chance to write something—anything—at a time when other kinds of writing seemed indulgent and superfluous. I'm not a political journalist, let alone an Arabist: I'm an idiot, or ιδιωτης, in its old Greek meaning of "private person," who clings to the belief that a private person writing on public events can see them in an importantly different way from the professional pundit, if only because he may be more alert to their private implications.

I hope these pieces can be read as an irregular personal diary of the period from September 11 to the beginning of George W. Bush's second term; a time when America moved, with startling speed, from a moment when it was extraordinarily united to a state of moral and ideological division not seen since—Vietnam? the Civil War? I've been visiting the US for more than thirty years and have lived here for the last fifteen: during the last four of those years, America, in its public and official face, has become more foreign to me by the day —which wouldn't be worth reporting, except that that sentiment is largely shared by so many Americans. The grammar and vocabulary of the language spoken by the administration and by a large segment of the news media differ so fundamentally from that spoken by people in my intellectual, political, and, as it happens, geographical neighborhood that debate between the two has become like the Englishman's idea of speaking a foreign language, which is to shout ever more loudly in his own. There's no possible negotiation between a phrase like "freedom and democracy on the march" and its cognate in the other language, "murderous chaos to which there is no foreseeable end." To that extent, *Hardball* and *Crossfire* are true mirrors of the present state of public discourse, and writing in this climate is a curious activity, since one knows that what might strike one reader as a mild statement of fact is likely to be read by another as treasonous—or in my case deportation-worthy—balderdash.

Some pieces are more political than others, and one may seem at first blush to be hardly political at all. The West Coast road trip described in "Termina Camino Rural," which began on the day that Condoleezza Rice began her testimony to the 9/11 Commission, was meant to be a no-radio, no-newspapers vacation, but it led my daughter and me into politics of another kind that implicitly bear on the obsessions of this book. For in the last four years the zillion tendrils of the war on terror have so grown to envelop us that they pervade everyday life, subtly and not-so-subtly changing its essential texture. The simple sight of a ship rounding the headland and entering the bay means something different now; so does the drone of an aircraft engine at an unexpected hour or off a usual flight path. A freight train, hauling at walking speed a string of pressurized tank cars through downtown on the Burlington Northern line, has a new and sinister significance. People look differently at strangers, especially swarthy strangers with accents, otherwise known as "men of Middle Eastern appearance."

Ferries, bridges, office towers rouse thoughts, however passing or dismissed as absurd, that would have been inconceivable four years ago.

The provisions of the Patriot Act extend to such hitherto unregarded actions as the checking-out of a book from the local library. Concrete barriers go up outside public buildings, supposedly meant to deter car bombers. Along the waterfront, loudspeakers, financed by the Department of Homeland Security, are in place, ready to order instant evacuation. Sniffer dogs, surveillance cameras, magnetometers, razor wire, BioWatch air-sampling devices, have become as familiar and unremarkable as stoplights and fire hydrants. In its role as theatrical impresario, the DHS has mounted a series of expensively produced mock terror attacks across the United States. None of this probably does much to hinder acts of real terrorism, but it all helps to assure us that we live in unprecedented times, a newly hazardous and frightening world, dependent on the long parental arm of government to shield us from our would-be killers.

Meanwhile the Bush administration's prosecution of the war on terror at home and abroad has drained attention and resources from other—just as pressing—issues. In January 2004, Sir David King, chief scientific adviser to the British government, wrote in *Nature* that "climate change is the most severe problem that we are facing today —more serious even than the threat of terrorism." A month later, a study by Peter Schwartz and Doug Randall, "An Abrupt Climate-Change Scenario and Its Implications for National Security," painted an extreme worst-case picture of flood, famine, and nuclear warfare, brought about by a sudden increase in global warming. What was primarily interesting about this paper was that it was financed, and released, by the Pentagon. What was secondarily interesting is that although it gained much notice in Europe, it was barely mentioned in the American press.

It's in ways like this that the war on terror increasingly distorts our view of the domestic scene. Under Bush's self-styled "wartime presidency," the composition of the American landscape is steadily altering. What was once in the foreground is moving into the background, and vice versa. Our world is being continuously rearranged around us in deceptively small increments. Though we like to pretend that the emerging new order is "normal," that daily life proceeds much as it always did, with a few small novel inconveniences, we keep on bumping uncomfortably into the furniture. It seems important to remember that this strange and disorienting redisposition of things is not the inevitable consequence of the September 11 attacks, but has been engineered by a political administration that could, and should, have responded to the attacks quite differently. For a sense of what alternative responses the Bush administration might have made, see the deeply thoughtful international colloquium, *Club de Madrid Series on Democracy and Terrorism*, published in June 2005 and available online at safe-democracy.org. It is a model of the kind of informed discussion that should have taken place in the United States before the Patriot Act was rushed through Congress, and in Britain before Tony Blair threatened a mass of hasty antiterrorist legislation in the month following the London bombings.

Lowell's "gloomy premonition" turns out to have been full of uncanny prescience. The greatest military power in history has shackled its deadly hardware to the rhetoric of fundamentalist Christianity, with all its righteously simplistic moralism, in a war of "good against evil" and "freedom against fear." Vietnam, though it was a terrible political and strategic miscalculation, was not like this. Yet American military iron is not an inexhaustible commodity, and even its piety, in the absence of all the promised miracles, looks now as if it just might be on the verge of running out.

I am grateful to the several editors who've allowed me space to spin out my thoughts in print: to Annalena McAfee and Ian Katz at *The Guardian*; Bill Buford, formerly literary editor at *The New Yorker*;

Simon O'Hagan and James Hanning at *The Independent*; Lee Froelich of *Playboy*; and, especially, Robert Silvers, who has let me write for *The New York Review of Books* on and off for just one year short of a quarter-century.

—Jonathan Raban, Seattle, August 2005

2

MY HOLY WAR

WHEN I WAS growing up in England, churches were still by far the tallest buildings in the landscape. With their towers and battlements, these domestic fortresses of Christendom, built as much to intimidate as to inspire, were close cousins and coevals of the Crusader castles in Turkey and the Middle East, like Birecik, Markab, and Crac des Chevaliers, whose lordly ruins I later saw, always from a distance and always with an unwelcome pang of déjà vu. My boarding school was attached to Worcester Cathedral, a magnificent crenellated pile, from the top of whose two-hundred-foot tower you could, so it was said, see clear across six counties. It was also said that a threepenny bit flipped out from the tower onto the head of an unwary passerby would cause instant death. This maneuver wasn't as easy as it may sound, and the cathedral roof below the tower was spattered with coins that had failed to reach their target, several of them mine.

The cathedral was full of emblems of Christianity's violent past. In the choir was King John's tomb, topped with a marble effigy of the King, brother of Richard the Lionheart, who taxed England dry to pay for his bloody Third Crusade against Saladin. In the south aisle, a museum case held a number of small treasures under dusty glass. I particularly relished a curled, yellowish-brown object that looked like a half-eaten cannoli shell. A faded label, inscribed in sepia ink, proclaimed it to be the skin of a flayed Dane. I never quite believed in children's hymns like "Gentle Jesus, meek and mild"; one had only to look around Christian buildings to see that this was a religion of the sword, of imperial conquest, of torture and coercion—a great, antique war machine, disguised as an engine of sweetness and light.

My father was a clergyman who came to ordination late, after a successful wartime career as an artillery officer followed by a spell as the regional secretary of a Christian voluntary organization. I was, from age twelve, a sullen atheist. Pimple-faced, voice treacherously skidding from baritone to falsetto, I tried to explain to my father that religion had always done more bad in the world than it had done good: What about the Spanish Inquisition? What about the Salem witch trials? What about the Thirty Years' War? What about the Bishops and the Bomb? It was obvious: religion was over—finished, a long disease for which the cure had been found in the form of mass education and a taste of modest material well-being. My father, in the yellowed dog collar that had seen service around my grandfather's neck and the ancient black cassock that had been passed on to him by my great-uncle Cyril, was an egregious (fast becoming my favorite word) anachronism, and might just as well have gone strolling around the village in codpiece and tights.

It was a lot easier to be a budding atheist in the mid-1950s than it was to be a budding vicar. The churches of England, grand as they appeared from a distance, were riddled with worm and rot. Beside each church stood a giant plywood thermometer, precariously rigged with guy ropes, recording the progress of the restoration fund for the tower or the roof. The thermometers often perished in the weather before the red paint began to climb the scale. Sunday congregations were thin and growing thinner—lost to TV, the home improvement craze, and weekend jaunts in the new family car.

After his curacy, my father's first full parish was a sprawling village, Pennington, on the outskirts of Lymington, in Hampshire. Luckily for him, the church was Victorian and not in a state of imminent physical collapse, and a fair sprinkling of parishioners still showed up at services. The local gentry came to Matins to set an example to the villagers, and because the church porch was their gathering point before they climbed into their Jaguars and Rovers and swept off for preluncheon sherry. The farmers came. So did the retired army types, who addressed my father as Padre, along with a dutiful remnant of shopkeepers and agricultural laborers.

Like most sixteen-year-olds, as I was then, I could see inside people's heads. None of the churchgoers actually believed. They might go through the motions, singing the hymns, crossing their hands to accept the Communion wafer, covering their eyes in the performance of public prayer, but they didn't really think that the world had been created by a Palestinian peasant, or that a personal paradise of harps and angels awaited them on the far side of their last visit to the Lymington hospital. These dark-suited hypocrites no more subscribed to my father's ritualist, Anglo-Catholic theology, with its transformational magic, than I did. I could tell, for I was an angry fundamentalist with a lock on truth, and as militant in my own way as any fanatic with a holy book. I could understand the idea of a Church Militant, but a church without passion, without conviction, without the steel of the true believer was beyond my adolescent comprehension.

It would be nearly twenty years before Philip Larkin wrote the lines that I wanted to quote to my father in 1958: "Religion.../That vast moth-eaten musical brocade/Created to pretend we never die." Even in rural Pennington, even on Sundays, we were on the brink of a new and saner world of secular realism. God would join the rest of our discarded toys up in the attic; the pretense of belief would be gone soon; and no one would ever again go into battle high on the hallucinogen of religious superstition. The idea that any religion would have sufficient power left in it to fuel a twenty-first-century war would have struck me as grotesque.

*   *   *

My father's second parish, to which he moved in the mid-1960s, was the kind of place that bishops describe as "a challenge"—a vast, shabby council estate, Millbrook, built by the city of Southampton to house its poorest citizens. The ugly purpose-built brick church was dwarfed by twenty-five-story tower blocks with vandalized elevators and urinous concrete stairwells, into which were packed new immigrants, single mothers, recidivists temporarily at liberty from their prisons, the unlucky, the feckless, the jobless, the chronically dependent. The windy shopping plaza at the center of the estate was largely untenanted. For some 20,000 people, there was a ladies' hairdresser, a liquor store, and a grocery smaller than the average American 7-Eleven.

The experience of ministering to this impossible parish radicalized my father. A lifelong reflex Conservative voter, he joined the Labour Party. His High Church theology became ever more attenuated and symbolic. He climbed his way through the tower blocks less as a priest than as a psychiatric social worker. He grew a beard that made him look like Karl Marx, left his dog collar in the drawer, and went about in an open-necked plaid flannel shirt. Although his church congregations were now tiny, he worked around the clock, negotiating with the authorities on behalf of his parishioners, succoring the needy, counseling the desperate, befriending the friendless.

In Millbrook, the Anglicans, the Catholics, and the Methodists were all in the same boat—down to the same dwindling, elderly band of congregants. My father's vicarage became an ecumenical center for the local clergy, fellow pilgrims in the stony landscape of twentieth-century unbelief. My mother served tea to the Methodists while my father shared his Haig whiskey with the Irish Catholic priest. Left out of these cheerful conferences were the proprietors of what my father called "tin tabernacles"—sectarians of unorthodox hue, like Spiritualists, Seventh-Day Adventists, charismatics, Pentecostals. I was now teaching the literature of the American Puritans, at a Welsh university college, and was getting professionally involved with serious theocrats, like Increase and Cotton Mather, whose take-no-prisoners style of religious practice struck a strangely warming chord in my atheistic, Marxist heart.

The despised tin tabernacles didn't appear to find Millbrook stony ground at all. There was always a good crowd on the balding grass outside the Pentecostal chapel on Sunday mornings, and many of the people there looked disconcertingly young. I had been taught to think of the wilder reaches of English nonconformity as marginal and eccentric, if not certifiably insane, and wrote off the Pentecostals as an irrelevant blip on the smooth graph of rising skepticism and declining superstition. The coming age of reason wouldn't be forestalled by ninety or so suburban enthusiasts, in puffy nylon golf jackets and raspberry-pink twinsets, talking in tongues. But I should have paid more attention. Millbrook was an issue, and so were tin tabernacles—small, disestablished powerhouses of vehemence and zeal. I made no connection then between the modern English illuminists and their American cousins and ancestors. Had I actually visited a tin tabernacle, I might have heard an echo of Jonathan Edwards preaching on "Sinners in the Hands of an Angry God," and realized that something was up—a new era of religious ferocity.

The leading players in the September 11 attacks found their vocations as fanatical holy warriors not in the God-fearing Middle East but in the most profane quarters of big cities in the West. Back home in Egypt, Lebanon, Saudi Arabia, their fathers, brothers, uncles have formed an incredulous chorus. "He was a donkey when it came to politics." "He was a normal person.... He drank alcohol, he had girlfriends." "His personality and his life bore no relation to the kind of things that happened." "We are in shock.... We thought he liked the USA." In Europe and the United States, each of these ordinary, insecure, unprepossessing men learned to think of himself as someone who might yet have a spectacular career, as a martyr. This peculiar strain of religious belief, with its equal measures of rage and passion for death, was hatched in Egypt more than fifty years ago, and seems to have found an ideal growing climate in exile, in the most secular-looking landscape yet devised: the low-rent, rootless, multilingual suburbs.

The essential charter of the jihad movement—its *Mein Kampf*—is Sayyid Qutb's *Milestones* (1964). Before Qutb toured the United States, between 1948 and 1950, he was best known as an Egyptian novelist, poet, and critic. After his time here, he became famous as an Islamic ideologue and a member of the Muslim Brotherhood, the Cairo-based think tank and home of theocratic revolution. He achieved martyrdom in 1966, when he was executed by Gamal Abdel Nasser. His book lives on. It can be found, in whole or in part, on many of the Internet sites created by Muslim students.

The heart of Qutb's argument rests on a rhetorical flourish: the modern world exactly reflects the state of things at the beginning of the seventh century, before the Koran was revealed to the Prophet Muhammad. The richest parts of Arabia were then occupied by foreign imperialists—Romans and Persians. Drinking, fornication, shopping, and vulgar entertainment were the chief pursuits of a morally bankrupt society sunk in *jahiliyyah*, the condition of ignorance, barbarism, and chaos from which the Arabs were providentially rescued by the gift of the Koran. They toppled their foreign oppressors and established the *khilafah*, or caliphate—that is, the nation (*ummah*) of Islam, which existed, though in steadily deteriorating form, until 1924, when the last caliph was deposed. The Sykes–Picot Agreement of 1916, in which the British and the French carved up Arabia into colonial spheres of influence, lent symmetry to the argument: history was on rewind, with the Romans and Persians walking backward onto the screen. The twentieth century was a new *jahiliyyah*, and the great project of the Islamic revival was the restoration of the rule of

Allah by force of arms. The coming jihad must be global in scale. Qutb wrote, "This religion is really a universal declaration of the freedom of man from servitude to other men and from servitude to his own desires. It is a declaration that sovereignty belongs to God alone and that He is the Lord of all the worlds."

Qutb didn't join the Muslim Brotherhood until 1952—three years after the assassination of the movement's founder, Hassan al-Banna, and two years after Qutb's spell of expatriation in the United States. Firsthand experience of Western *jahiliyyah* seems to have transformed Qutb from a devout but orthodox believer into the architect of worldwide jihad. His American writing (fragments of it were translated and published by John Calvert in 2000 in the journal *Islam and Christian-Muslim Relations*) shows him as a lonely naïf, adrift in a world of lewd temptations. Although Qutb was forty-two when he sailed from Alexandria for New York in 1948 (the Farouk regime was paying him to study American education methods), his voice sounds painfully young. On the voyage out, a "drunken, semi-naked" woman showed up at the door to his cabin, an American government agent, dispatched by Langley expressly to corrupt him—or so he told his Egyptian biographer years later. Qutb's sense of extreme moral precariousness comes to the fore in every encounter. Few men past the age of forty can ever have felt their immortal souls to be in such danger at a church hop as Qutb did when he attended one in Greeley, Colorado. The pastor, doubling as disk jockey, lowered the lights to impart "a romantic, dreamy effect," and put on a record of "Baby, It's Cold Outside" (presumably the Esther Williams and Ricardo Montalban version, from the soundtrack of the 1949 hit movie *Neptune's Daughter*). "The dancing intensified.... The hall swarmed with legs.... Arms circled arms, lips met lips, chests met chests, and the atmosphere was full of love." We're in the psychodrama of temptation here —the language tumescent with arousal, even as it affects a tone of detachment and disdain.

In his Koranic commentary, *In the Shade of the Qur'an*, Qutb suggested that the believer's brief sojourn on earth should be spent "purifying the filthy marsh of this world." Rich, sexy, Truman-era America gave him a taste of this world at its filthiest and marshiest. His American letters show him wading fastidiously, a lone pilgrim, through "the life of *jahiliyyah*, hollow and full of contradictions, defects and evils." American jazz, football, wrestling, movies (though he confessed to enjoying *Gone With the Wind* and *Wuthering Heights*), the talk of cars and money supplied Qutb with ammunition for his great theological assault on "this rubbish heap of the West"; and so did the dedication of his Greeley neighbors to weekend lawn maintenance. America, with its natural disposition to clamor and excess, has always been a happy hunting ground for puritans of every denomination; Qutb scored a notable first when he hit on lawn mowing as a target for a spiritual critique of the West. But sex, not lawns—shameless, American, *jahili* sex—was clearly uppermost on the mind of this lifelong bachelor. The word "desire" ripples through *Milestones*, and always, it seems, meaning the same thing—the drunken temptress on the ship, a tattooed boy in a Washington, D. C., coffee shop, the terrible peril of the church hop.

The Muslim Brotherhood's Hassan al-Banna, who attempted to liberate Egypt from its corrupt "apostate" monarchy, had told his followers to "prepare for jihad and be lovers of death." It is easy to see death's erotic allure for a man of Qutb's temperament, raised on the Koran's worldly and sensual depiction of the hereafter. The Gardens of Bliss resemble nothing so much as the great Playboy Mansion in the sky, watered by underground springs (all sorts of delightful wetness abound in Paradise), and furnished with cushions and carpets designed for life on the horizontal. Male entrants are greeted by "companions"—"maidens, chaste, restraining their glances, whom no man or jinn before them has touched." Qutb insisted that the descriptions of Heaven in the Koran were symbolic, not literal. The pomegranates wouldn't really be pomegranates, nor the maidens really maidens. These "luxuries...similar to luxuries enjoyed in this life" were there to "help us to imagine the ultimate of sweetness and joy." Yet the Koranic Paradise remains obdurately earthbound, full of nubile girls unzipping plantains. It reads like the dream of a repressed and awkward man who might be a young soldier on a foreign posting, or Sayyid Qutb in Greeley, Colorado, or Mohamed Atta in Harburg, Germany.

Like many homesick people, living outside their language in an abrasive foreign culture, Qutb aggrandized his loneliness into heroic solitude. Walking the streets of Greeley, he was the secret, lone agent of God's will. In *Milestones*, there's a passage that is unmistakably a portrait of Qutb in America: "The Believer from his height looks down at the people drowning in dirt and mud. He may be the only one; yet he is not dejected or grieved, nor does his heart desire that he take off his neat and immaculate garments and join the crowd." Being able to look down on people drowning in dirt and mud makes you feel taller, the better to "enjoy" your faith as you survey the obscene couplings of the little folk who roll in the ordure below.

This is exactly the posture that hard-line Islamists who live in the West today are advised to adopt. Web sites and magazines of the radical Muslim diaspora are preoccupied to the point of obsession with the issue of "living with *kufr*." *Kufr*—a simpler notion than *jahiliyyah* —is disbelief; *kuffar* are unbelievers or infidels. "It is a fact of life that we must, to some extent, keep close company with the *kuffar*. This is almost unavoidable given that we work, study, and unfortunately play with them," Amir Abdullah wrote in an article entitled "Preserving the Islamic Identity in the West: Threats and Solutions," published in the magazine *Nida'ul Islam*, in the spring of 1997. "The likeness of Islam and *kuffar* is like that of fresh clear spring water and water brought up from the bottom of a suburban sewer. If even a drop of the filthy water enters the clear water, the clarity diminishes.

Likewise it takes only a drop of the filth of disbelief to contaminate Islam in the West."

Kufr leaks through the TV set into Muslim homes, bringing "moral bankruptcy" to the living room, turning children against parents, wives against husbands: "The news provides us with an insight into the world around us. A world where mujahideen are called 'terrorists,' where the Straight Path is called 'Islamic Fundamentalism,' and where all Muslims are misogynistic wife-bashers." The *kuffar* lie in wait for tender innocents: "Muslim families, having lost much of their Islamic values, have sold out to the West. By sending our children to kindergarten and child care centers, we are sending our children to be suckled by the *Shaytan*" (Satan). Or, as the title of an article on One Ummah (a mainstream Muslim Web site, and no great friend to radical Islamism) puts it, "Do You Know What *Shaytan* Is Feeding Your Baby?"

Nida'ul Islam, which I take to be the *New Left Review* of the Islamist revolution, is published in Lakemba, a nondescript low-rise suburb nine miles southwest of downtown Sydney, and aims to reflect "the Jihad stream amongst the Islamic movements." Long, admiring interviews with Sheikh Omar Abdel Rahman and Osama bin Laden run alongside political analyses of "apostate" regimes in Muslim countries (the Sauds, Mubarak, Qaddafi, Hussein, Musharraf), extracts from *Milestones*, and advice columns on topics like adjusting to college, shaving the beard, what to do about Christmas, and choosing a wife. The magazine consistently represents the life of the Muslim in the West as a hazardous survival exercise in enemy-occupied territory. *Kufr* is an oppression as real as any Middle Eastern tyranny. In some ways, it's even more dangerous to live among the *kuffar* than in, say, Fahd's Arabia or Mubarak's Egypt, because the forces of *kufr* are more insidious and omnipresent. *Shaytan* stalks the suburbs, trying to catch believers off guard. A Christmas card arrives in the mail. Someone from the office invites you to have a drink with him after work. Your daughter begs to be allowed to go to the prom. You find your own eyes straying to the window of the adult lingerie store. You had better remember your Sayyid Qutb:

> There is only one place on earth which can be called the house of Islam, and it is that place where an Islamic state is established and the Shari'ah is the authority and God's laws are observed.... The rest of the world is the house of war.

Collaboration with the enemy will result in punishment in the hereafter. If, for instance, you cast your vote in a *kufr* election, you commit the mortal sin of *shirk*—which is to associate other gods or rulers with Allah. Last June, when the rest of the British press were busy endorsing Tony Blair or William Hague, the monthly *Khilafah Magazine* published a special election issue in which it endorsed God. As Qutb said, "A Muslim has no nationality except his belief."

What is loosely called the Muslim world has given its inhabitants ample experience of oppression; of constant surveillance by the secret police and their informers; of jail, torture, summary execution performed as a fête champêtre in the market square. (In 1978, I saw—or, rather, heard—two men shot like this in front of a large and eager crowd in Sanaa, Yemen; Polaroid pictures of their exploding heads were hawked, minutes later, as valuable souvenirs.) Many of the key texts of Islamic revolution were written in exile, in hiding, or in a prison cell. A consciousness forged in conditions of tyranny is liable to find tyranny wherever in the world it settles—in Haldon Street, Lakemba, or in Gloucester Road, London SW7. Islamism—which by no means signifies Islam at large—needs oppression. A powerful sense of *kufr* helps the believer to live in Western exile in the necessary state of chronic persecution, from which his theology was born, and on which its survival depends.

It also confers a heroic glamour on the everyday alienation felt by the immigrant—especially the male immigrant—who struggles to keep his head up in a foreign culture. The American who condescends to you because she doesn't understand your funny accent is not simply being bad-mannered; she's evil—an agent of *Shaytan*. Your corrosive solitude is the measure of your invincible superiority to the *kuffar*, in their hellbound ignorance and corruption. You are not as they are. You make a point of not shaking hands with the female examiner of your thesis. When the next-door neighbors toss a ball that happens to roll across your path, you walk on without looking up. At Shuckum's Raw Bar and Grill, you loudly put down the barmaid in a row over the $48 tab. At Huffman Aviation, you grab the seat cushion belonging to another student, and refuse to give it back. These are not displays of sullen adolescent aggression; they're moral gestures, designed to put the *kuffar* in their rightful place. It's what certain angry, frustrated young men have always secretly dreamed of—a theology of rebellion, rooted in hostility and contempt.

Since the deposition of the last caliph, in 1924, Islam has had no one to speak with authority on its behalf. It relies instead on a quarrelsome army of jurists and scholars, each of whom interprets the Koran, the Sunna (stories of the Prophet's exemplary life), and the Hadith (the Prophet's sayings) according to his own lights, which leads to a marvelous profusion of schisms, sects, and heresies. We've had a taste of this in recent months, as various scholars (a generously inclusive term) have construed the meaning of the word "jihad" for a Western audience.

There is greater jihad (Jihad al-Akbar) and lesser jihad (Jihad al-Asghar), and total impassioned disagreement as to which is which. Is greater jihad an internal struggle against one's own desires? Or is it war, on a literal battlefield, against the *kuffar*? For every moderate imam who categorically states that it is the first, there's a radical Islamist who argues, with equal plausibility, that it's the second. The best you can discover about the "true" meaning of "jihad" is that you were a fool to ask the question in the first place.

We know to our cost what the word means to "the jihad stream," though we seem to be hopelessly ignorant of the width and depth of that sectarian branch of the Islamic river. American Muslims of the kind who agree to be interviewed by reporters invariably say that it's a piddling and heretical rivulet, while Osama bin Laden and his claque boast that it's more on the scale of the Amazon or the Nile. It has found its way into virtually every major Western city. It is taught by charismatic mullahs in hundreds of suburban Islamic tin tabernacles, like Sheikh Omar Abdel Rahman's community mosque in Jersey City and Abu Hamza al-Mazri's mosque in Finsbury Park, London. Several of the suspects in the September 11 attacks were said to have plugged into it on the Internet from their lodgings in Florida and San Diego. Marwan al-Shehhi and Mohamed Atta found it in a tiny improvised mosque in Harburg, across from Hamburg on the wrong side of the Elbe.

One thing I have in common with Mohamed Atta is a longstanding affection for the Aleppo souk, about which he wrote his thesis at Hamburg-Harburg Technical University. I spent seventeen days in Aleppo in the 1970s, with no other commission than to lose myself in that maze of ripe-smelling underground streets and limestone tunnels, each one dedicated to a single commodity—gold, hides, soap, transistor radios, rugs, spices, plastic toys, ouds (the Arabic ancestors of the lute), canned vegetables, silks, rope, copperware, shoes. Walk far enough in the Aleppo souk, navigating with your nose, and you'd eventually find any object you could name. I checked with Google to see just how long the souk actually is, if all its streets were laid end to end, and found it to be, variously, seven, eight, ten, twelve, thirteen, sixteen, and "about 30" kilometers. That haziness corresponds exactly with my memory of the place, which is geometrically contained and yet has a labyrinthine infinitude. It can be walked through in a few minutes, or it can go on forever. Lit with strings of flyspecked low-wattage bulbs, it is—or was—an Arabia in miniature; a lovely, complex urban organism that had, when I was there in 1978, gracefully collapsed the twentieth into the fifteenth century. Tourism in Syria then amounted to little more than the occasional busload of Soviet factory workers, though Aleppo outside the souk was becoming an untidy mess of concrete and cinder block, its narrow streets choked with drivers who kept their thumbs permanently on their horns.

Twenty years later, Mohamed Atta saw the souk as being under siege by tourists and their architecture of fast-food restaurants and multistory hotels. One glance at a picture of the 250-room Chahba Cham Palace, a memorably ugly brute that now towers over Aleppo, is enough to make me warm to Atta's thesis that the souk is dying, fatally polluted by the Western-style developments that surround it.

In Harburg, as Atta meditated on the poisoning of Aleppo, he found his way to the al-Tauhid mosque, where the anti-American Islamist theology of the imam made a snug fit with Atta's academic pursuits. The particular object of Atta's abomination was the American skyscraper—the global symbol of the insolent power of the *kuffar*. His thesis topic couldn't have been better chosen to illustrate the dark preoccupations of the jihad stream: in the Aleppo souk, Atta had found an age-old, smelly world of half-lit arched passages, violated by shameless and greedy *kufr* intruders—an image that might spring straight from the pages of Sayyid Qutb, where sex and jihad are intimately entwined.

Atta's architectural ideas, his displacement in the wilderness of outer Hamburg, and his growing fury at the apostate regime in his native Egypt, combined with an acute sexual squeamishness, all coalesced with the paranoid Koranic scholarship of the al-Tauhid mosque, and he resolved to contribute his life to the cause of Allah. It's the business of religion to put two and two together and make five. The dialectic of purity and pollution led him to the "noble obligation" of martyrdom. He let his beard grow. He took to scraping the frosting off cakes, lest it contain lard. His manner changed from smiling and polite to the frigid altitude of the believer, stepping fastidiously through the filth of *kufr*. He went missing for the duration of 1998, a period most likely spent in an al-Qaeda training camp in Afghanistan.

Ministering to the alienated and the displaced, my father wore his beliefs thin to the point of transparency. The idea that alienation and displacement might themselves constitute the basis of a religious awakening would have been repellent to him. Broad Church Anglicanism was about reaching out to the margins to reclaim people for the center: born in political compromise, the Church of England had little appetite for protest and none for rage.

"Woe to the bloody city of Lichfield!" George Fox, the first Quaker, shouted as he walked barefoot through the town in 1651. You'd never catch a member of the Anglican clergy doing that. Fox wrote proudly of the "mighty dread" that his preaching inspired, and of the fear of the citizens when they learned that "the man in leathern britches has come." Like his hat, which remained defiantly stuck to his head when he was indoors, the leather gear was an outward sign of Fox's spiritual estrangement from the depraved world of seventeenth-century England. Fox and his original Quakers (the "new fanatic sect, of dangerous principles," as John Evelyn described them in his diary in 1656) might have created a real stir in Millbrook; but my father, going about the parish in plain clothes, with his increasingly plain-clothes theology, had little to offer to the angry, the excluded, the exploited, the male young.

As I see now, my own atheism—my ultimate weapon in the Oedipal war—was really a dissident religious creed, full of furious conviction and an inchoate, adolescent hunger for the battlefield. It went hand in hand with membership in the Campaign for Nuclear Disarmament (CND). The first time I entered my father's Pennington vicarage wearing the three-legged runic peace symbol on my lapel, it met with an immensely satisfactory response: "I will not have your wearing that badge in this house." From then on, I was a nuclear fundamentalist.

I waylaid girls and frightened them with the deadly poetry of kilotons, neutrons, gamma rays, fallout, and radiation sickness. At one mile . . . at two . . . at five. As my father had the Gospels, so I had the bomb. I used it daily, to make mushroom clouds all over Hampshire and to gain converts to my brand of millennialism. The box of badges that I kept in my bedroom rapidly emptied. I secretly indoctrinated my younger brothers, aged nine and ten, telling them that God was finished and that we were at world's end, unless I and my kind won out against the deaf, blind, stupid old men of the establishment, like the vicar of Pennington, who were leading us down the path to certain annihilation.

CND was then led by John Collins, the "Red Canon," a renegade Anglican priest of whom my father richly disapproved, and the ancient, spry, pixieish Bertrand Russell, atheism's own philosopher-king. The organization must have been embarrassed by its militant-extremist faction—the young men of warrior age for whom the peace symbol was a regimental badge and CND their rampaging army.

Each Easter, we marched—out of step and out of uniform, but marched—in loose platoons, under rippling banners, from Aldermaston, site of the Atomic Weapons Research Establishment, to Trafalgar Square, sleeping rough and living off the land like guerrillas. For mile after rainy mile, we sang "The Red Flag":

> *The people's flag is deepest red*
> *It shrouded oft our martyred dead;*
> *And ere their limbs grew stiff and cold*
> *Their hearts' blood dyed its every fold*

I can still feel the intense warming glow of unearned righteousness that accompanied the singing of these words. Midway between Bracknell and Windsor, standing shoulder to shoulder with the world's oppressed, voicing our hatred of the belligerent power of the United States and its puppet nations in the NATO alliance, we were bathed in personal glory:

> *Then raise the scarlet standard high!*
> *Beneath its shade we'll live and die.*
> *Though cowards flinch and traitors sneer*
> *We'll keep the red flag flying high!*

Back at the vicarage, my father blew a gust of St. Bruno pipe smoke over the remains of breakfast, and said, "So you think Mr. Macmillan needs to take moral guidance from a bunch of spotty teenagers, do you?" Nothing like a traitor's sneer to harden belief into the steel of true zealotry: I finished him off with a single round from my thought-murder gun.

Lately, I've been keeping that angry boy on hand, to read the literature of jihad on my behalf. As skeptical as I am, he nevertheless reports with a scowl that he can connect with it pretty well. As, perhaps, he should. He was an unwitting participant in the fervor. It was his father who was the less deceived. The vicar of Pennington, later rural dean of Southampton, went to his grave a rationalist, a stoic, a rueful humanist in a world ablaze with passionate supernatural convictions.

The running cliché about the Afghan war is that it is a conflict between a "modern" and a "medieval" worldview. The reassuring implication is that its outcome is a foregone conclusion. Although Mullah Omar and his immediate colleagues did look as if they'd escaped from the cast of a production of *Ali Baba and the Forty Thieves* (their retro

fashion itself a telegenic political statement), the wider jihad movement is not a benighted relic of the Middle Ages but a modern construct, built and operated by thoroughly modern young men.

The first reported British casualties in this war were amateur
soldiers from Luton, Crawley, Leicester, and London who had en-
listed with the Taliban and were promptly claimed as martyrs by the
Tottenham-based Islamist organization al-Muhajiroun (the Emigrants). The suburban mujahideen were second-generation English-
men, several of them university-educated, who sacrificed the prospect
of well-paid secular careers for their shot at Paradise. In Lahore,
Abdul Momin, a twenty-five-year-old civil engineer from east London, bound for Kabul, told a reporter from *The Observer*, "I did not
like London because it is spiritually rotten. I want to live a proper
Muslim life." In Luton, a young Muslim told *The Guardian*, "Lots of
us believe that it is right to fight against the Americans and the British,
even if we have grown up in Britain."

Trooping off to find their corner of a foreign field, in much the
same spirit as an earlier generation went to Spain with the International Brigade, the volunteers were Web designers, engineers, students,
delivery drivers. They came across as cool, wired types, as comfort-
able in their modernity as any of their fellow surfers in the Internet
cafés. So did Mohamed Atta, Hani Hanjour, Ziad Jarrah, and the
other hijack suspects, who left a forensic spoor of brand names across
the length and breadth of the United States. We know them best as
efficient modern consumers—of Parrot-Ice, Tommy Hilfiger, Econo
Lodge, AAA discounts, Starbucks, CyberZone, Golden Tee '97 golf at
Shuckum's Raw Bar and Grill, Salem cigarettes, Heineken and Bud-
weiser, Chinese takeout from Wo Hop III, lap dancing at Nardone's
Sports Go-Go Bar and the Olympic Garden Topless Cabaret.

There's nothing unmodern about a worldview that recoils from the
spiritual emptiness of the urban-industrial West. Sayyid Qutb began

Milestones with the observation that Marxism and capitalism were in a state of terminal moral exhaustion:

> The leadership of mankind by Western man is now on the decline, not because Western culture has become poor materially or because its economic and military power has become weak. The period of the Western system has come to an end primarily because it is deprived of those life-giving values which enabled it to be the leader of mankind.... At this crucial and bewildering juncture, the turn of Islam and the Muslim community has arrived.

Spengler and Toynbee stand conveniently at Qutb's elbow, to aid and abet the coming revolution. The bankrupt West has failed mankind. The present cycle is coming to its inevitable end. Now it's Islam's "turn."

If *Milestones* exhibits an intense, prurient disgust at the fallen morals of the modern city, berates the present with allusions to the splendors of the ancient past, prophesies the end of Western civilization, and holds up religion as the purifying force in a contaminated world, it's in distinguished company, for these are also the essential themes of *The Waste Land*, the archtext of literary modernism. At least one radical Islamist is on record as having been a T. S. Eliot fan —Fathi Shiqaqi, the leader of the Palestinian Islamic Jihad, who was assassinated in 1995—and it's not hard to see how Eliot's characteristic preoccupations could chime with those of the decline-of-the-West jihadis. It would appall Eliot, the Anglo-Catholic churchwarden, to hear it, but his vision of a society collapsing into spiritual ruin is very close to what Qutb tries to conjure in his depiction of *jahiliyyah*. The moral indictment of the West, central to the Islamist case, has impeccable Western credentials.

*   *   *

Far from being antiquated or alien, most of the intellectual baggage of the jihad movement, like the lifestyle of its guerrillas, is disconcertingly familiar. It's like seeing a stranger sitting at the wheel of what you always thought was your car. A photograph of one of the British volunteers for service with the Taliban showed him in a T-shirt blazoned with the slogan "The Final Revelation, the Final Message, the Final System, the Final Conquest: Islam"—a message as modern in its way as the medium that carried it.

Recently, much solemn incredulity has been expended on the case of John Walker, the "American Talib." Closely echoing the male relatives of the hijack suspects, Walker's father, a lawyer, said, "I can't connect the dots between where John was and where John is." Yet given the twin American traditions of experimental religiosity and tireless self-reinvention, the dots don't seem all that far apart. On one level, at least, Walker appears to have led an almost mythical American life in its seemingly frictionless transformations: earning his high school diploma at sixteen, converting to Islam (via hip-hop and the Internet) after reading *The Autobiography of Malcolm X*, becoming a fluent Arabist in Yemen, then a devout jihadi at a Pakistani madrasah—before he then became a guerrilla in Kashmir and Afghanistan. His evolving identity required a succession of new names—Suleyman al-Lindh, Suleyman al-Faris, Abdul Hamid. With family money, an appetite for travel, a pious idealism, a quickness of mind, and extraordinary cultural adaptability, this son of Marin County is a recognizable version of a classic American type, of the kind who might have been found on the road to Marrakech or Ladakh, or hanging out with Peruvian revolutionaries—and never more so than when, interviewed on his stretcher by CNN, he was found to speak English with a distinct Arabic accent. "My heart became attached to them," he said of the Taliban, as if translating from a finer, more eloquent language than the one to which he was born. Seeing Walker, and his commonsensical Catholic father, I was sent into a spin of uncomfortable recollection.

Instead of prosecuting Walker for conspiring to kill Americans, the United States authorities might more usefully install him in a university somewhere and turn him into a research project. Psychologists, theologians, political scientists, and cultural historians could then sit at his feet and draw him out on the subject of why the call to jihad answers so resonantly the yearnings of clever, unhappy, well-heeled young men, from Mill Valley and Luton as well as from Cairo and Jidda. What he says might be more alarming than anything to be found in the caves of Tora Bora, and a lot more difficult to defeat.

—February 2002

3

HERE WE GO AGAIN

SOMEWHERE IN THE letters home of Gertrude Bell, the doughty English archaeologist and colonial administrator, there is a description of a pleasant afternoon spent riding in the Mesopotamian desert in 1918 or 1919. Bell trails a walking stick in the sand. Behind her, Arab boys erect cairns to mark the future boundary between what will eventually become the states of Iraq and Saudi Arabia.

Bell was one of the many British and French nation-builders who carved up Arabia in the years following the Sykes–Picot Agreement of 1916. The lines they drew in the sand rarely corresponded to any preexistent historical, tribal, cultural, or geographical reality. The nations they invented were arbitrary agglomerations, their borders thrown up around dozens of warring local sheikdoms. These fictional states were given kings (the British loved to create monarchies in their own image) and elegantly written constitutions, as if the right sort of ceremonial language and regular twenty-one-gun salutes could somehow transform the chaos of post-Ottoman Arabia into a neat patchwork of Denmarks, Hollands, and Swedens with date palms and minarets.

A nation so fancifully constructed does not easily lend itself to governance. You need a warlord, with a loyal standing army and a far-flung force of secret policemen, to prevent the country from falling into the turmoil that is the natural state to which it is perpetually tending. The systems of government that have evolved in Syria, Iraq, and Saudi Arabia are paranoid family dictatorships with ancestral roots in a single city or village. Thus the Assad family of Qurdaha, an Alawite village up in the hills behind Latakia, Syria's Mediterranean port. Thus the Saud family of Riyadh, an oasis town in the Nejd desert, now the capital of Saudi Arabia. Thus the Husseins of Tikrit, a town ninety miles north of Baghdad, and the birthplace of Saladin. (Saddam's full name is Saddam Hussein al-Tikriti.)

If the European inventors of these countries believed that generously drawn borders would encourage a commensurate enlargement of national as opposed to local consciousness, the effects have been quite the reverse. To be an army general, a security chief, or a government minister in Arabia, it is necessary to come from Qurdaha, Riyadh, or Tikrit, and better still to bear the name of Assad, Saud, or Hussein. So the village, and the family and clan, supply a tyrannical ruling class which treats the rest of the country as an unruly empire, to be held in place, as empires are, by regular shows of military and terroristic power. In the case of Syria and Iraq, the reigning families belong to religious minorities: the Assads are members of the eccentric Alawi sect, though most Syrians are Sunni Muslims; the Husseins are Sunnis, and Tikrit is a Sunni enclave in Shiite Iraq.

The least unstable states in the Arab world are emirates that have survived intact from long before Picot and Sykes arrived on the scene. They too are family businesses. The al-Sabahs of Kuwait, the al-Khaleifas of Bahrain, the al-Thanis of Qatar, the al-Nahyans of Abu Dhabi, and the al-Maktoums of Dubai have been in power for around two hundred years. But these functioning political entities are tiny. Qatar, for instance, is roughly the size of Devon and Cornwall combined, with a third of their population; its neighbor Saudi Arabia, by contrast, is nearly five times the size of France.

The Sauds, Assads, and Husseins practice a form of rule that works well enough in a tiny country such as Qatar, but is a disaster when applied on a larger scale. It fills prisons and graveyards and breeds among its subjugated peoples the kind of impotent despair and fury that makes them natural candidates for conversion to Islamist totalitarianism.

Consider the case of Hama in Syria, a city famous for its huge, groaning waterwheels (they are said by the local poets to make a sound like that of women in orgasm). It is a center of Sunni conservative puritanism, always hostile to the secular Baathist regime of Hafiz al-Assad. In 1982, a group of Sunni militiamen ambushed an army patrol in the heart of the old city, and sparked an Islamic uprising against the provincial government. Assad sent in the Syrian army under Alawite commanders. Most of Hama was flattened. Between 10,000 and 25,000 Hamaites, most of them civilians, were slaughtered.

It is an important axiom of the Bush administration that Saddam has used weapons of mass destruction "against his own people"; but the concept of "own people" in Arabia needs footnoting, as the Hama massacre illustrates. When Assad sent his army into Hama he was not moving against his "own people" so much as attacking his traditional enemies, whose base lay within his territorial jurisdiction. So it was with Saddam and the Kurds, and Saddam and the Shiites. From the perspective of Tikrit, the Kurdish city of Halabja and the floating villages of the Shiite Marsh Arabs did not contain Saddam's own people: they were, rather, insolent colonial outposts that needed to be taught a savage lesson.

In the Middle East, the concept of nationality is understandably weak: it would be hard to feel patriotic allegiance to the capricious lines in the sand traced by Bell and her kind. To say "I am a Syrian" or "I am an Iraqi" means a lot less than to say "I am a Damascene" or "I am a Baghdadi." For the ancient cities of Arabia—Cairo, Jerusalem, Damascus, Aleppo, Baghdad, Mecca, Medina, and Sanaa—used to have the character of Renaissance city-states, as grand or grander than Venice and Florence. Even now, when you go to, say, Aleppo or Sanaa, you can feel their political self-containment as a once great center of civilization and commerce. A powerful sense of the civic, as it relates to people's hometowns, is matched by something very close to indifference to the national, and no amount of enforced flag-waving and protestations of fealty to the dictator in make-believe elections is going to change or conceal that fact of Arab life.

Yet one vastly potent nationalism haunts the Arab world: the idea of the *ummah*, the nation or community of believers. It is to the *ummah* that Osama bin Laden addresses his calls for armed resistance to the West and its "puppet" dictators in the region. Notice that he never speaks of "Saudi Arabia," his own home country; he always refers to it as "the land of the two holy mosques," for to bin Laden and his followers the Saud family are usurpers, kept in place by the patronage and military might of the US. In Osama's version of things, the country we know as Saudi Arabia exists only as a piece of arrogant colonial mapmaking. Notice that in his most recent audiotape he spoke of "our sons in Iraq"—meaning not Saddam and his Tikriti henchmen, whose secular Baathist regime has long been on his hit list, but the faithful millions who live inside the artificial borders imposed on Mesopotamia by the Western powers when they summoned Iraq into being.

It is hard for us to understand the intoxicating appeal of pan-Arab Islamic nationalism—the dream of an Arabia without borders, united under a restored caliphate, answerable only to Koranic law, the Sharia. To Western eyes, Sharia law, with its public stonings, beheadings, amputations, its male triumphalism, appears tyrannical in the extreme. How could anyone see in it the promise of liberation?

The answer lies in the despotic tyranny under which most Arabs now live. President Bush said, "They hate us for our freedoms," but that is not true: freedom is a rare commodity that Arabs would dearly like a lot more of. They hate us, rather, for the condition of humiliating subjection in which they find themselves, and for which, rightly or wrongly, they hold us responsible. They hate us for Sir Mark Sykes, for Georges Picot, for Gertrude Bell, for Arthur James Balfour (whose 1917 "declaration" was the basis of the movement to create a Jewish state in Palestine); for America's steadfast support of what they perceive as corrupt and cruel regimes (like that of the Saud family in its glittering hi-tech fortress of modern Riyadh) and for its bland indifference to the injustice suffered by the Palestinians.

All this may be unreasonable of them, but that is why they hate us, and that is why, in the poorest parts of Arabia, the favorite name to give a boy at present is Osama: the latest folk hero of an impossible, idealized "Islamic nation" that will transcend the petty frontiers of the hopelessly divided and despotic Middle East. This is not meant to sound soft on bin Laden: he is a monster, but a monster born of desperate dreams that are widely shared across an immense and unhappy tract of land.

Now we are going nation-building in Arabia once again. No one in the present US administration seems to have any useful memory of our earlier adventures in this department, and no one appears able to clearly distinguish between the two crucially different bad-hats with sallow complexions, Osama bin Laden and Saddam Hussein. No one seems to have noticed that toppling Saddam, though it ranks a good deal lower on the agenda than toppling the Sauds, is a necessary part of Osama's larger game plan. We are on the brink of an intervention that will rank in Arabian history beside the Sykes–Picot Agreement and the Balfour Declaration, and we are bringing to that intervention a terrifying mixture of ignorance and amnesia.

—November 2002

4

PACIFIC OVERTURES

"US Public Hardens Behind War
But Radical Fringe Finds Its Voice"
—headline in *The Guardian*, March 12, 2003

NOT TRUE—or at least not true in my corner of the US, where the leafiest and richest suburbs are thickly placarded with NO IRAQ WAR signs, and where, on weekend protest marches against the Bush White House, prosperous bourgeois families, more usually seen tramping around the downtown art galleries on the first Thursday evening of each month, hugely outnumber the bearded peaceniks of the radical fringe.

A few days ago, Speight Jenkins, the general director of the Seattle Opera, said that in the course of a season of heavy fund-raising he hadn't so far encountered one person who was in favor of the war: fringe radicals are not usually people who can fork out seven-figure checks to keep the Ring cycle going. At the private elementary school attended by my daughter, NO IRAQ WAR bumper stickers adorn the Range Rovers and Toyota Land Cruisers of the soccer moms, along with slyer, milder protest slogans, such as CARTER FOR PRESIDENT IN '04." At dinner parties and public meetings earlier this week, the mood was pitched somewhere between aghast hilarity and downright despair as Seattle waited for a war in which it appears to want no part at all.

Some of this might be put down to simple provincial isolationism: squatting on its deep backwater of the Pacific, walled in by mountain ranges, 2,800 miles from Washington, D. C. (known here, without affection, as "the other Washington"), Seattle is congenitally suspicious of enthusiasms hatched inside the Beltway. But its view of the larger world is shaped by a different ocean. When Seattle's sleep is disturbed by geopolitical bad dreams, it is more likely to be visited by the specter of Pyongyang (to which it is the nearest big city on the American mainland) than Baghdad. For Seattle, militant Islamism begins in Indonesia, not North Africa or Arabia, and Indonesian container ships dock at a terminal which, from the point of view of an al-Qaeda operative, is conveniently located right next to the downtown business district. The city is a potential sitting duck, for terrorist dirty bombs as for North Korean nuclear warheads, but the threat posed by Saddam Hussein and his WMDs seems remote.

Seattle is a liberal Democratic stronghold. The Seventh Congressional District, which includes the city and a good chunk of its suburbs, is a constituency so comfortably settled in its voting habits that the congressman from Seattle can afford to voice left-leaning opinions that would have most of his House colleagues quickly booted from office. The present incumbent, now in his eighth term, is a cheerfully uninhibited ex–child psychiatrist named Jim McDermott, who has been known as Baghdad Jim since last autumn, when, interviewed on live network television from Iraq, he lectured America on the number of infant deaths caused by sanctions. He seems to rejoice in the nickname. The state's senior senator, Patty Murray, born and raised in the Seattle suburbs, got into big national trouble when the Drudge Report publicized her meeting with a group of high school students in Vancouver, Washington, where she asked the kids to consider the very Seattleish question of why Osama bin Laden should be widely regarded as a folk hero in the Middle East. (Answer, he invested in the local infrastructure in Sudan, Yemen, and Afghanistan, and "we haven't done that." For a few days, all hell broke loose on the right-wing talk-radio stations.) Long ago in the 1930s some wit remarked that there were the United States of America and the Soviet of Washington State, and Seattle likes to deliver occasional reminders that it was once the headquarters of the Industrial Workers of the World, the Wobblies—as it did in 1999 with the WTO demonstrations.

That said, Seattle is by no means antiwar in general. It houses the main plant of Boeing, the company that made the city rich in the Second World War. It's ringed with large military bases—the naval air base on Whidbey Island, naval bases at Everett and Bremerton, the army base of Fort Lewis and the McChord Air Force Base near Tacoma—and military spending of one sort and another puts $8 billion a year into the Washington state economy. There has been an almost-daily slot on the local TV news for pictures of tearful farewells on the bases as the forces deploy for the Gulf, and of toddlers waving handkerchief-sized American flags at the receding sterns of aircraft carriers sailing north up Puget Sound. The signs saying SUPPORT OUR TROOPS and NO IRAQ WAR are complementary rather than oppositional. It is this war for which Seattle has no stomach.

Theology comes into it. When I first moved here, I cherished the fact that Seattle has one of the lowest churchgoing rates in the nation, and when it does go to church, it likes its religion to be on the cool and damp side—Lutheran, Catholic, or Episcopalian, for preference. On his Web site, McDermott cautiously admits that he "attends" the Episcopalian cathedral of St. Mark's, which diplomatically excuses him from owning up to any particular belief, or disbelief, in God.

President Bush, who talks of his relationship with Jesus as if they'd been Deke fraternity brothers in college and casts himself as God's personal instrument in the war against evil, may warm the hearts of his Bible Belt supporters, but he offends in Seattle, where Christian, hardly less than Islamic, fundamentalists tend to be viewed as people who've taken a good thing a great deal too far. In this reserved, northern, Protestant (though not that Protestant) city, Tony Blair's moral eloquence on Iraq meets with a kind of puzzled admiration, while Bush's narrow televangelical fervor arouses much mistrust, for he speaks in a language more often associated here with charlatans than with honest pastors. To the Seattle ear, George Bush sounds an awful lot like Jimmy Swaggart.

If that applies to Bush, it applies even more strongly to the secular absolutists and visionaries by whom he is surrounded—and especially to Paul Wolfowitz and Richard Perle, who pop up everywhere, propounding the case for invasion. God doesn't specifically figure in Wolfowitz's big-picture vision of a born-again Arab world, but the terms in which his great plan is phrased are both religiose and fundamentalist. In Wolfowitz's version of the domino theory, democracy is a contagion, spreading through the Middle East after the (effortless) conquering of Iraq. Iran...Syria...Saudi Arabia...state after state goes down with democracy, as with flu, each falling on the next with a gentle click. Establish Connecticut-on-the-Tigris and the rest follows with an inexorable logic of the kind that operates only in dreams and revelations. It is all, as Bush would say, "faith-based."

It will also cost us little or nothing. I lost a couple of hours sleep a few days ago, when at 11:30 PM I switched from the local news to C-SPAN and happened on Wolfowitz answering questions from a captive audience in a California think tank. With the glint of fanatic certitude in his eye, he was explaining how both the invasion of Iraq and its reconstruction would be comfortably paid for by its own oil supplies. Win-win. A no-brainer.

Listening to him, I thought: This kind of talk comes two years too late for Seattle.

For the city is going through a phase of chastened realism. Until the Nasdaq began its long slide in March 2000, taking the stocks of local companies like Amazon and RealNetworks down to pathetic fractions of their previous value, Seattle was on a delirious roll and full of true believers in the magic of the New Economy, which generated profit from loss and made instant millionaires of everyone with 5,000 or 10,000 stock options. For Seattle, the dot-com boom was a reprise of the Klondike gold rush in the 1890s, which funded the building of most of the landmark "historic" (this is a young city) houses and office blocks in town. It set off another wave of grandiose construction, much of it still waiting to be occupied and paid for.

FOR SALE signs have given way to ones saying FOR RENT. Hotel lobbies have an eerily deserted air. Restaurant tables go begging, and many once packed joints have given up and closed their doors. The erstwhile paper millionaires are keeping busy mailing out their résumés, for the Seattle area, which at the turn of the millennium had one of the most buoyant economies in the nation, now heads the nation's unemployment rates. This isn't meant to suggest that Seattle now looks like, say, the urban northeast of England in the early 1980s, with the mass closure of coal mines and factories: there's still an enormous amount of wealth concentrated here. But since March 2000 the city has been digesting the hard lesson that money does not, as it once did, grow on trees.

Once bitten, twice shy. Having just breathlessly stepped off the roller coaster of the New Economy, Seattle is wary about being taken for another ride aboard the New World Order. The Wolfowitz scheme for the market democratization of the Middle East rather closely resembles the kind of untested business plan for which venture capitalists here used to hand over millions of dollars without a second thought in the heady days when the Internet was going to make supermarkets redundant and Seattle's household chores were all going to be performed by MyLackey.com. (When MyLackey went broke, it was said that its biggest problem was that few people had any clear idea as to what a lackey is or was.) Seattleites are thoroughly familiar with the strategy of Shock and Awe: you have to begin with a massive "burn rate" to establish a "global footprint," at which point the enterprise begins to pay for itself "exponentially." Except that most such enterprises ended up filing for Chapter 11 bankruptcy protection, and so did the venture capitalists who funded them.

It used to be a point of Seattle principle that every spectacularly successful venture begins life in somebody's garage. You had only to say the word to evoke the spirit of Jeff Bezos and Amazon. That's true no longer. One thing seriously wrong with Wolfowitz's business plan is that it bears all the marks of having been cooked up in a garage.

Seattle has two daily newspapers. Ownership of *The Seattle Times* is split between the Knight Ridder publishing empire and a local family, the Blethens. The *Seattle Post-Intelligencer* is owned by the giant Hearst Corporation, which is hardly famous for its liberal bias. In October 2000, the *Times* narrowly endorsed the presidential candidacy of Bush for his "civility," "integrity," and understanding of "the dynamics of taxes, regulations and enterprise that form a successful business." The *Post-Intelligencer* endorsed Gore, for his "experience, knowledge, and philosophy," and "because we have grave misgivings about the breadth and depth of Bush's grasp of the essential knowledge required of the president and commander in chief of the world's sole superpower." Neither paper is politically predictable. Though the *Post-Intelligencer* generally sits somewhat to the left of the *Times*, both papers usually endorse a fairly equal number of Republicans and Democrats. Both are now severely critical of the Bush administration, and one has squarely opposed the invasion.

After the President gave his brink-of-war press conference on March 6, 2002 ("This is the last phase of diplomacy..."), the *Post-Intelligencer* editorial board took a communal deep breath and announced themselves unpersuaded by Bush's case:

> We were eager for clarity and precision—and it was not to be....
> Bush...has left us discomfited.... We, like many Americans,

remain unconvinced of the direct connection between al-Qaida and Iraq, or that Iraq presents a clear and present danger to us.

The editorial ended: "'It's time for people to show their cards,' Bush said. We're left wondering if he really understands the stakes."

The *Times*, in keeping with its business-minded endorsement of Bush in 2000, attacked the President for his evasive accounting procedures:

> The Bush administration is dodging the cost of war with Iraq as studiously as Saddam Hussein is hiding chemical and biological weapons.... The administration is running a tab without disclosing what the costs have been.... The White House obviously suspects its figures might complicate support for the war. That is a politic instinct, but it is inappropriate in a democracy that thrives on information. It is also just plain wrong.

The subtext here is that Washington, like many other states, is this year facing a massive budget shortfall, requiring deep cuts in education, health, child care, and policing. The National Governors Association recently put out a report saying that "nearly every state is in fiscal crisis." So the prospect of America's hitherto untraveled President going abroad, at taxpayers' expense, on an adventure of untold, untellable cost, comes at a singularly bad moment for the individual states—and especially for Washington, whose New Economy tax base has been steadily shriveling over the last two years. In basic housekeeping terms, Seattle and the White House are living in different worlds.

Over at the *Post-Intelligencer*, where resistance to the war is rooted more in mistrust of its moral and political objectives, the most heartfelt and persistent criticism of the administration has come from David Horsey, the paper's Pulitzer Prize–winning cartoonist, whose drawings of the forty-third president show him as a scrawny, simian-featured homuncule with a childish predilection for dressing up; now as Caesar, now as Napoleon, as a western gunfighter, as a tin-hatted soldier-hero from the Normandy beaches. Caught in private, in plain shirt and khakis, Horsey's George Bush resembles the unprepossessing night clerk in a convenience store—a Walter Mitty figure, ridiculously too small for his office. Horsey took a year off to study international politics at the University of Kent, Canterbury, and his cartoons are more conceptually elaborate than most. Here, for instance, is Bush the huckster-showman, wielding a distorting fun-house mirror to vastly magnify the small, torpid rat labeled Saddam Hussein, and inquiring of his audience, "Are you scared enough yet?" Here's bin Laden on his prayer mat, addressing a shopping list of requests to God, and finding that George W. Bush is the answer to all his prayers. Here's Bush in the same position, coming to the bewildered conclusion that God must be a Frenchman.

In "Leader Without a Compass," Horsey depicts Bush as a pith-helmeted adventure-tour guide, dragging an unwilling young woman named America, unsuitably dressed in beach-vacation wear, through a jungle infested with dangerous beasts, of which much the least threatening is the sleepy crocodile of Iraq. In "The Bush Victory Garden," the tender seedling of Afghan democracy has died in a landscape of cracked mud, while the thistles of opium farming, warlords, and al-Qaeda are in vigorous bloom. Bush looks up from a creased map of Iraq to ask Kim Jong Il, who is perched on the nose cone of a North Korean warhead: "Say! Do you know a good back road to Baghdad?"

On a local note, "Every Party Needs a Pooper" has a roomful of pie-eyed inebriates, drunk on war, being visited by Congressman McDermott holding a pot of coffee labeled "Inspections First." For Christmas, Horsey drew two children dreaming in their beds: the American child dreamed of Santa coming down the chimney; the

Iraqi child dreamed of an American missile taking the same route. I've seen angrier cartoons in the British press, but none that offer such a thoughtful range of reasons for dissent. Horsey's work can be seen on www.seattlepi.com/horsey.

One measure of the *Post-Intelligencer*'s emerging position on the war is that, since Tuesday, it has started to run Robert Fisk's reports for *The Independent*. Fisk! His skepticism about US intentions in the Middle East sets him apart from all other British, let alone American, correspondents; it is as if the *Post-Intelligencer*, after listening to Bush's address to the nation on Monday night, had turned to Jacques Chirac for a more enlightened view of things.

The United States is the least monolithic country on earth, and you're bound to get a skewed picture of the nation at large from inside the perspective of just one of its myriad quarrelsome constituencies. From where I live, there appears to be no very significant gulf between American and European opinion: as far as I can fairly judge it, Seattle's position on the invasion of Iraq differs little from that of, say, Bristol or Manchester, or even Hamburg or Lyon, though it is seriously out of sync with that of Washington, D. C. Yet Seattle does not believe itself to be on the radical fringe—and I have a hunch that I'd be writing in a very similar vein if I were living in Des Moines, Iowa, or any one of a dozen provincial capitals in the US.

Suspicion of the national polls has hardened into outright disbelief. "You can get a poll to say any damn thing you want," McDermott said the other day; but there's more to it than that. In the climate of John Ashcroft's new security state, the question "Do you support the President's policy on Iraq?" asked over the phone by a faceless pollster easily mutates in the mind of the citizen to "Are you a patriot?" or even "Do you want to get in trouble?" As Bush has put it: Either you are with us ... And in the wake of September 11 it troubles Americans to own up to being against the administration. Which does not mean they are for it.

There is also much anger at the Democrats for failing to provide any articulate leadership in the war on (not with) Iraq. To many of its traditional supporters, the party appears to have been gutlessly complaisant in its bipartisan stance. But something interesting happened on February 21, when the present crop of presidential hopefuls paraded in front of the Democratic National Committee in what several reporters likened to a beauty pageant. Joe Lieberman made a speech so flat that his candidacy may well have died in that moment. Richard Gephardt boasted of making common cause with the Bush administration on Iraq, and was met with cries of "Shame!" but went on to outline his domestic policy and won a series of standing ovations. Then came Howard Dean, the former governor of Vermont:

> I'm Howard Dean, and I'm here to represent the Democratic wing of the Democratic Party.... What I want to know is why in the world the Democratic Party leadership is supporting the President's unilateral attack on Iraq.

Dean's opening remarks were enough to leave both Lieberman and Gephardt in the dust. The hall was in an uproar of approval and relief. At last a reasonably qualified and plausible presidential candidate was saying something that rank-and-file Democrats have been waiting to hear for many months. The immediate upshot of his speech (by no means limited to the war) was an orgy of text messaging from state delegates to their party officials back home, saying that Gephardt had rescued himself after a bad start, Lieberman had flopped, and Dean had carried the day gloriously, on the economy as much as on the invasion of Iraq. Dean is far from being a Gene McCarthy figure; he comes with a raft of policies, one of which happens to be about the war. In the last month he has moved from being an utterly obscure figure to anyone not from Vermont, to being a neck-and-neck front-runner in the Democratic nomination race. If this has come as a surprise to most national political commentators, it doesn't seem at all surprising if you happen to live in Seattle.

"We Are All Americans Now": *Le Monde*'s headline on September 13, 2001, has been much quoted as a reminder of how disastrously the Atlantic alliance has broken apart in the course of the last eighteen months, and of how wantonly the Bush administration has squandered the world's goodwill toward the US. Yet living here, far from the Beltway, I'm struck by how many Americans have become no less alienated than the great mass of British, French, Belgian, or German voters by the American government's stand on Iraq. A few days ago, the *Post-Intelligencer* ran an editorial headlined (with no irony at all intended) "Vive la France, Friend and Ally." On this issue, a surprising number of Americans feel they are Europeans now.

As cruise missiles and laser-guided bombs dive on Baghdad, public opinion will inevitably harden in favor of the administration, and will further solidify when the first remains of American servicemen are brought back to the US—in body bags, if they've been killed by conventional weapons, in urns if they've fallen to biological ones. Yet there will still fester the sense that this is a grossly unaffordable war, an immoral war fought on a policy wonk's fantastic premise that "democracy" can be imposed by brute force across the Middle East. In six months' time, I doubt that convictions now so widely held in this West Coast city will be seen as the property of a radical fringe. Watch Howard Dean.

—March 2003

5

THE GREATEST GULF

WHATEVER ITS IMMEDIATE apparent outcome, the war on Iraq represents a catastrophic breakdown of the British and American imagination. We've utterly failed to comprehend the character of the people whose lands we have invaded, and for that we're likely to find ourselves paying a price beside which the body count on both sides in the Iraqi conflict will seem trifling.

Passionate ideologues are incurious by nature and have no time for obstructive details. It's impossible to think of Paul Wolfowitz curling up for the evening with Edward Said's *Orientalism*, or the novels of Naguib Mahfouz, or *Seven Pillars of Wisdom*, or the letters of Gertrude Bell, or the recently published, knotty, often opaque, but useful book by Lawrence Rosen, *The Culture of Islam*,[1] based on Rosen's anthropological fieldwork in Morocco, or Sayyid Qutb's *Milestones*. Yet these, and a dozen other titles, should have been required reading for anyone setting out on such an ambitious liberal-imperial project to inflict freedom and democracy by force on the Arab world. The single most important thing that Wolfowitz might have learned is that in Arabia, words like "self," "community," "brotherhood," and "nation" do not mean what he believes them to

---

1. University of Chicago Press, 2003.

mean. When the deputy secretary of defense thinks of his own self, he—like me, and, probably, like you—envisages an interiorized, secret entity whose true workings are hidden from public view. Masks, roles, personae (like being deputy secretary of defense) mediate between this inner self and the other people with whom it comes into contact. The post-Enlightenment, post-Romantic self, with its autonomous subjective world, is a Western construct, and quite different from the self as it is conceived in Islam. Muslims put an overwhelming stress on the idea of the individual as a social being. The self exists as the sum of its interactions with others. Rosen puts it like this: "The configuration of one's bonds of obligation define who a person is...the self is not an artefact of interior construction but an unavoidably public act."

Broadly speaking, who you are is: who you know, who depends on you, and to whom you owe allegiance—a visible web of relationships that can be mapped and enumerated. Just as the person is public, so is the public personal. We're dealing here with a world in which a commitment to, say, Palestine, or to the people of Iraq can be a defining constituent of the self in a way that Westerners don't easily understand. The recent demonstrations against the US and Britain on the streets of Cairo, Amman, Sanaa, and Islamabad may look deceptively like their counterparts in Athens, Hamburg, London, and New York, but their content is importantly different. What they register is not the vicarious outrage of the antiwar protests in the West but a sense of intense personal injury and affront, a violation of the self. Next time, look closely at the faces on the screen: if their expressions appear to be those of people seen in the act of being raped, or stabbed, that is perhaps closer than we can imagine to how they actually feel.

The idea of the body is central here. On the Web site of Khilafah .com, a London-based magazine associated with the international Islamist organization Hizb ut-Tahrir, Yusuf Patel writes: "The Islamic Ummah is manifesting her deep feeling for a part of her body, which is in the process of being severed." It would be a great mistake to read this as mere metaphor or rhetorical flourish. *Ummah* is sometimes defined as the community, sometimes the nation, sometimes the body of Muslim believers around the globe, and it has a physical reality, without parallel in any other religion, that is nowhere better expressed than in the five daily times of prayer.

The observant believer turns to the Ka'aba in Mecca, which houses the great black meteorite said to be the remnant of the shrine given to Abraham by the angel Gabreel, and prostrates himself before Allah at *Shorooq* (sunrise), *Zuhr* (noon), *Asr* (mid-afternoon), *Maghreb* (sunset), and *Isha* (night). These times are calculated to the nearest minute, according to the believer's longitude and latitude, with the same astronomical precision required for sextant navigation. (The crescent moon is the symbol of Islam for good reason: the Islamic calendar, with its dates for events like the Haj and Ramadan, is lunar, not solar.) Prayer times are published in local newspapers and can be found online, and for believers far from the nearest mosque, a $25 Azan clock can be programmed to do the job of the muezzin. So, as the world turns, the entire *ummah* goes down on its knees in a never-ending wave of synchronized prayer, and the believers can be seen as the moving parts of a universal Islamic chronometer.

In prayer, the self and its appetites are surrendered to God, in imitation of the Prophet Muhammad, the "slave of Allah." There are strict instructions as to what to do with the body on these occasions. Each prayer time should be preceded by ritual ablutions. Then, for the act of prostration and the declaration of "*Allahu Akbar*" (God is great), the knees must touch the ground before the hands, the fingers and toes must point toward Mecca, and the fingers must not be separated. Forehead, nose, both hands, both knees, and the underside of all the toes must be in contact with the ground. The body of the individual believer, identical in its posture to the bodies of all other believers, becomes one with the *ummah*, the body of the Islamic community on earth. The abdication of self five times a day, in the company of the faithful millions, is a stern reminder that "self-sufficient" is one of the essential and exclusive attributes of Allah, mentioned many times in the Koran. Human beings exist only in their dependency on each other and on their god.

The physical character of this prayer is unique to Islam. Jewry and Christendom have nothing like it. The *ummah*, a body literally made up of bodies, has a corporeal substance that is in dramatic contrast to the airy, arbitrary, dissolving, and reconstituting nations of Arabia. To see the invasion of Iraq as a brutal assault on the *ummah*, and therefore on one's own person, is not the far-fetched thought in the Islamic world that it would be in the West.

For weeks *The Jordan Times*, like every other newspaper in the region, carried front-page color pictures of civilians killed or wounded in Operation Iraqi Freedom. Government censorship being what it is, these photographs could afford to be more eloquent and candid than the stories printed beneath them. On April 2, the picture was of an Iraqi father in a dusty gray jellaba, arms spread wide, screaming at the sky in grief, while at his feet, in a single bare wood open coffin, lay huddled the three small, bloodied bodies of his children. His rage and despair can be seen exactly mirrored in the faces of Egyptian demonstrators in Tahrir Square, as the *ummah* bewails the injuries inflicted on it by the Western invaders. Geographical distance from the site of the invasion hardly seems to dull the impact of this bodily assault.

It's no wonder the call of the *ummah* effortlessly transcends the flimsy national boundaries of the Middle East—those lines of colonial convenience, drawn in the sand by the British and the French eighty years ago. Wolfowitz repeatedly promises to "respect the territorial integrity" of Iraq. But integrity is precisely what Iraq's arbitrary borders have always lacked: one might as well talk about respecting the integrity of a chain saw, a pair of trousers, and a blancmange.

When the British cobbled together Iraq out of three provinces of the collapsed Ottoman Empire, they were deliberately fractionalizing and diluting two of the three main demographic groups. It made good colonial sense to split up the ever-troublesome Kurds (Sunni Muslims, but not Arabs) between Syria, Turkey, Persia, and Iraq. Equally, the Shias had to be prevented from dominating the new state. In her letters home, Gertrude Bell, an archaeologist and official of the British administration in Baghdad after the First World War, described the Shias as, variously, "grimly devout," "violent and intractable," "extremist," "fanatical and conservative." By contrast, the Baghdad Sunnis were seen as generally docile, forward-looking, and pro-British. A representative democracy was out of the question, because the majority Shias would promptly hijack it. Bell wrote: "I don't for a moment doubt that the final authority must be in the hands of the Sunnis, in spite of their numerical inferiority, otherwise you'll have a mujtahid-run, theocratic state, which is the very devil." (Wolfowitz, please note.)

Out of the lawless turmoil of liberated Iraq there emerged one image of placid civil order: a photo, taken in April 2003 and published in *The New York Times*, showing some seven hundred Basra Shias seated in neatly serried rows outside their damaged mosque, listening to a sermon. This in a city otherwise given over to riot, looting, and murder. The contrast between the power of the occupiers and the power of the ayatollahs could not have been more forcefully stated.

Bell and her colleagues sent for Faisal—son of the emir of Mecca—who had already had a go at being king of Syria before the French deposed him. As a member of the Hashemite family, direct descendants of the Prophet, Faisal, though a Sunni, was acceptable to the Shias. So the perils of democracy were neatly circumvented. Bell again:

> Lord! They do talk tosh. One of the subjects that even the best of [the Arabs] are fond of expatiating upon is the crying need for democracy in Iraq—al damokratiyah, you find it on every page. I let them run on, knowing full well that Faisal intends to be king in fact, not merely in name, and he is quite right.

From the start, the unwieldy assemblage of Iraq needed not a government but a ruler. When monarchy failed, tyranny of a peculiarly Middle Eastern kind took over. Rosen interestingly asserts that the idea of "state," in the Western sense of a complex machinery of government independent of the person of the ruler, barely exists in the Arab world, because an entity as abstract and impersonal as a state cannot be credited with those "bonds of obligation" that define and constitute the Islamic self. This is borne out by fundamentalist Web sites that warn their followers not to vote in Western elections for fear of committing the sin of *shirk*, or blasphemy: to show allegiance to a secular state, instead of to the *ummah* and to Allah, is to worship a false god. The typical Arab ruler is likely to echo Louis XIV: the state, such as it is, is him—a warlordlike figure on a grand scale, with an army and a secret police at his disposal, like Gamal Abdel Nasser, Hafez al-Assad, King Saud, or Saddam Hussein. For the individual strong man is compatible with strict Islamist teaching in a way that a strong state is definitely not.

In the case of Iraq, arrogant colonial mapmaking happened to conspire with Islamic tradition to create a state that would permanently tremble on the verge of anarchy, or at least of violent partition into a Kurdistan to the north, a Shiite theocracy to the south, and a Sunni-led secular statelet in the middle with Baghdad as its capital. That Iraq still conforms—just—to its 1921 borders is a tribute to the extraordinary power and brutality of Saddam. Yet Wolfowitz has singled out this state-that-never-should-have-been for his breathtakingly bold experiment in enforced American-style democracy. On April 6, 2003, he went the rounds of the Sunday-morning talk shows to "warn" the nation that it might take "more than six months" to get Iraqi democracy up and running. He should be so lucky. What seems to be happening now is that as American troops take full possession of Iraq, they are beginning to find out—in Baghdad, Ur, Mosul—that the country they invaded has effectively ceased to exist.

Beware of the *ummah*. Never has the body of believers been so vitalized by its own pain and rage. The attacks on Gaza and the West Bank by Israeli planes and tanks, the invasion of Afghanistan, and the invasion of Iraq are seen as three interlinked fronts of the same unholy project. Each magnifies and clarifies the others. Pictures of American troops in Baghdad are eerily identical to those of Ariel Sharon's army in Gaza City, right down to the black hoods and white plastic cuffs used by both Americans and Israelis on their prisoners. Likewise, the bloody corpse of a Palestinian child appears in the same front-page space on Wednesday that on Tuesday was occupied by the bloody corpse of her Iraqi cousin.

Just as the American invasions of Afghanistan and Iraq gave the Sharon regime cover for fresh reprisals against the Palestinians, so they have given the Palestinians themselves a global context for their struggle. The image of overwhelming Western military force bearing down on an oppressed Muslim people, once local and particular, is now general. Two weeks ago, at a massive demonstration in Alexandria, the crowd moved through the streets chanting: "America and Israel are one enemy, Iraq and Palestine, one cause."

That such demonstrations are happening at all, in places where political demonstrations are normally instantly disbanded by armed riot police, is a measure of how even the repressive tyrants of the Middle East are having to bend to the fury of their people. Hosni Mubarak, who presides over a country that is constantly threatening to erupt in an Islamist revolution, warned that the American action in Iraq would "create a hundred bin Ladens." Since the invasion began, Mubarak has had to tolerate criticism of his regime in the Egyptian newspaper *Al-Ahram*, which is a little like Khrushchev taking criticism from *Pravda*. Similarly, King Abdullah has been seen on Jordanian national television, defending his fence-sitting policy against a barrage of questions that showed scant respect for his regal person. All these might, of course, be seen as welcome signs of "liberation," although it's doubtful if Wolfowitz ever meant to liberate the Middle East in order to bring the rights of free assembly and expression to millions of enraged theocrats.

On April 7, Fahed Fanek wrote in the usually mild-mannered *Jordan Times*:

> What can the world do to confront the overwhelming superiority of the US air force? Nothing more than face up to it with hatred of America, its policies and the Bush administration. It is possible that the weapon of hatred will prove more effective and more enduring than that of the American air force.

Don't mistake the tone here. Fanek is no advocate of the hatred he describes. Yet hatred of America is becoming so deeply ingrained in the essential character of Arabia that even America's friends in the region, like Fanek, are having to write of it as a governing fact of Arab life, as incurable as weather.

For the first three weeks of Operation Iraqi Freedom there was extraordinary unanimity in the way the story was handled in English-language newspapers across the region, as by Islamist Web sites around the world. Every downed American helicopter and captured American tank was a trophy to be gloated over. Every Iraqi casualty was a brother or sister to be mourned. Every day when Allied progress was apparently slowed or halted was celebrated as a cause for pan-Arab, pan-Islamic pride. "Muslims of Iraq Greet the Crusaders with Bullets Not Flowers" was a representative headline. Government-controlled newspapers, usually regarded by the Islamists as craven lackeys of America's puppet rulers in the region, were very nearly of one voice with the hard-line jihadist Web sites. One such site, run by al-Muhajiroun (the Emigrants) in London, has a grisly photo-feature under the jeering title of "BBC: 'We Are Winning.'" The pictures that follow are close-ups of dead and horribly wounded Allied troops, weeping Allied POWs, and wrecked Allied military hardware, interleaved with sarcastic quotations from members of the Bush administration, like "This will be a campaign unlike any other in history," "There's pockets of resistance, but we're making good progress," and "It is a breathtaking sight to see it." Yet what is most striking is that al-Muhajiroun, followers of Sheikh Omar Bakri Muhammad and his colleague, the one-eyed, hook-handed Abu Hamza, are now only slightly out of step with the mainstream Arab press, where most of the photographs made their first appearance, and were meant to carry the same message.

The invasion seems, ominously, to have moved Osama bin Laden from the margin to the center. It is his words that keep surfacing—like "crusaders," which first came to wide public notice in "Jihad Against Jews and Crusaders," the freelance fatwa issued by bin Laden in February 1998. There he wrote:

> The Arabian peninsula has never—since Allah made it flat, created its desert, and encircled it with seas—been stormed by any forces like the crusader armies spreading in it like locusts, eating its riches and wiping out its plantations. All this is happening at a time in which nations are attacking Muslims like people fighting over a plate of food.

Seven years after the first Gulf war, this sounded overblown and out of date. Now, with an American military occupation pitched in Iraq for an indefinite period, the extravagant phrasing has taken on an unexpected kind of realism. So too with "crusaders." Then, in the obsessively memorious way of Arabia, it quaintly harked back nine hundred years; now it conjures the fundamentalist Christian zealotry of the Bush administration and its religiose war on "evil." And calling the invading forces "crusaders" serves another function: it dissolves distinctions of nationality and creates an anti-*ummah*, a malign global body of unbelievers, with all the unanimity of purpose and conviction attributed to the *ummah* itself.

After September 2001, an immense quantity of effort was put into the discovery, or creation, of the elusive and precious link between the Iraqi regime and bin Laden's al-Qaeda organization—a task that defeated all the best American and British alchemists. It took invasion to bring the link into being. Now it's there in full view, as sturdy a piece of ironmongery as anyone could wish for, with "Made in America" stamped all over it. In the last few weeks, bin Laden's cause has acquired a degree of legitimacy that would have been inconceivable a year ago. Our dangerous new world is one in which seeming rhetorical embellishments are fast morphing into statements of literal fact, and Mubarak's forecast of a hundred bin Ladens could turn out to be a serious underestimate.

Beware triumphalism. On the day that Allied troops crossed the border from Kuwait into Iraq, a CNN reporter named Walter Rodgers was to be seen "embedded" in an Abrams tank. Rodgers is what Americans call "an older man," but aboard the tank, in the company of boys from the "Seventh Cav.," he appeared to have regained his lost youth, in all its callow swagger and bounce. Prattling exultantly about the deadly potency of his big 120mm gun, Rodgers rode off into the desert, a gravel-voiced, ash-haired Tom Sawyer on a romantic teenage escapade.

His reporting gave deep offense. The next day, a CNN correspondent based in Qatar told how a Palestinian friend of hers in Beirut had expressed alarm at the "gee whiz" style of the network's coverage of the invasion—clearly a reference to Rodgers. Once, jingoistic news broadcasts were received only by the domestic audiences whose morale they were designed to boost. Now, when Walter Rodgers growls into the mike that he and his boys are going to "bite a chunk off Baghdad," he can be heard and seen by Islamists around the world as the living embodiment of America in her war of conquest and revenge.

On September 11, 2001, Americans were sickened by the image of Palestinians dancing in a Jerusalem street, in demented jubilation at the collapse of the World Trade Center. Beamed from one world into the homes of another, the cheering celebrants appeared subhuman—not people but a whooping pack of Tasmanian devils at the kill. There have been moments in the American cable TV coverage of the Iraq invasion when that image has come uncomfortably to mind. "Sickened" is a fair description of the tone of the English-language Arab press as it has contemplated both the war itself and America's apparent gusto for it. So familiar a revulsion ought, surely, to command recognition from us, but America has treated Arab opinion with haughty indifference, dismissing it—when it condescends to notice it at all—as standard-issue "anti-Americanism," that reflexive grouchiness which tends to afflict anyone unlucky enough not to carry a US passport.

On television, the Iraqis themselves have been relentlessly feminized and infantilized, exactly along the lines described in Said's *Orientalism*. They are the Little People: all heart and no head, creatures of impulse and whim, not yet grown-up enough to make rational decisions on their own behalf. Surveying a scene of bloody chaos in Mosul, with gunshots exchanged between gangs of looters, the Fox News reporter indulgently observed that all this was only to be expected, because "their emotions have been so bottled-up, after thirty years of dictatorship." Ah, yes.

Children need fathers, and the person appointed by the US (the Pentagon, to be precise) to act in loco parentis to the unruly young Iraqis is someone perfectly typecast to administer the smack of firm paternal government. The retired general Jay Garner is a defense missile contractor ("arms dealer" in the Arab press) and close associate of Wolfowitz, Defense Secretary Donald Rumsfeld, and Vice President Dick Cheney, whose best-known political avowal was his signature of the "Flag and General Officers' Statement on Palestinian

Violence" put out by the Jewish Institute for National Security Affairs in October 2000:

> We, the undersigned, believe that during the current upheavals in Israel, the Israel Defence Forces have exercised remarkable restraint in the face of lethal violence orchestrated by the leadership of a Palestinian Authority that deliberately pushes civilians and young people to the front lines.
>
> We are appalled by the Palestinian political and military leadership that teaches children the mechanics of war while filling their heads with hate....

Unsurprisingly, the Jewish weekly *Forward* welcomed the news of Garner's appointment with the headline "Pro-Israel General Will Oversee Reconstruction of Postwar Iraq." Unsurprisingly, the news incensed the Arab world—as, no doubt, it was calculated to do, for the selection of Garner was nakedly triumphalist and entirely in keeping with the Bush administration's policy of teaching the Middle East a humiliating lesson.

Here's another metaphor that could turn literal. Last September, Amr Moussa, secretary-general of the Arab League, said if the United States invaded Iraq it would "open the gates of hell." Florid arabesque or fair warning? We shall soon find out.

—April 2003

6

SECRET STATE

I WOKE UP on Thursday morning to the voice of Richard Perle, talking on National Public Radio about how to "win" the "War on Terror." Among a string of alarming proposals was his suggestion that Americans "associated with" "terrorist organizations" should be stripped of their citizenship so as to liberate them from any inconvenient rights they might have to the protection of US law. My quotation marks are, I'm afraid, a sign of the times. One needs to handle the language now with a pair of tongs, gingerly picking up each official phrase as if it were a potential explosive device. Welcome to America under the Patriot Act, where dozens of formerly innocent words are suspect, and none more so than the word "security."

As a visitor to the US, you won't much enjoy being fingerprinted, photographed, and asked to supply a "biometric" passport; nor will you relish being shooed away from the toilet on the plane because where two or three are gathered together they might constitute a terrorist cell. But these measures are out in the open, and if you can read about them in newspapers they are by definition the public window dressing that the Department of Homeland Security wants you to see. It's the covert that truly threatens us, and America, once famous for the openness of its government, has under the Bush administration become the most secretive state in the history of modern peacetime democracy.

But we are, of course, "at war," and have been so since the President declared one in the immediate aftermath of September 11. (The al-Qaeda attacks on the World Trade Center and the Pentagon might have been treated as a massive criminal act, and prosecuted accordingly; it was George Bush's choice to label them as warfare.) Certainly the menace of terrorism is real—and has intensified since the invasion of Iraq and the consequent inflammation of Islamist rage against the US. There's every reason to assume that an American—or a British—city will be the target of militant Islamists armed with a dirty bomb, or a supply of ricin or anthrax, or in possession of an airliner heavily laden with explosive aviation fuel, or... we have no idea of the timing or the method, which leaves us very effectively terrorized.

So the secrecy is justified. The government knows more than we do. What we don't know is for our own good. Leave it to the administration. Trust Daddy. Close to half of the voting-age population in America appears to subscribe to that view, while the other half fears that democracy itself is being fatally undermined by the administration's unseemly eagerness to exploit every available political possibility of this war (which isn't quite a war) on terror (which, as an abstract noun, is unlike any enemy ever caught in the sights of a sniper's rifle).

Living in Seattle, I've seen and felt the American climate alter steadily and for the worse over the last twenty-eight months. Degree by degree, it's getting colder. Old Glory is hoisted proudly on the flagpoles of pro-Bush houses and condos, while paranoia and conspiracy theories fly ever higher in the flagless ones. "Security" is a partisan issue, as when, just before Christmas, Tom Ridge, the head of Homeland Security, announced that he'd upped the level of alert from yellow to orange and that the threat of terrorist attack on the mainland United States was "greater now than at any point since September 11, 2001."

Obviously Ridge couldn't tell us how he knew this—that would be in breach of security. Yet his department did let drop that "chatter" had been heard—and there's another word whose innocence is forever gone. It was for "chatter" that warplanes buzzed American cities over Christmas, Coast Guard gunboats stood on watch in harbors, flights from abroad were canceled or escorted into American airspace by more warplanes, and plainclothes operatives roamed the streets with portable radiation detectors, looking for traces of cesium 137 in the Yuletide air. The vast and cumbersome apparatus of security was taken out of the secret closet and given some no-doubt-useful exercise.

Only paranoid conspiracy theorists, or liberal Democrats, would go so far as to insinuate that an administration which has misled the public, or been plain wrong, on so much else—on the "link" between Saddam Hussein and al-Qaeda, on weapons of mass destruction, on the cost of war, on how toppling Saddam would instantly liberate the infectious germ of democracy in the Middle East—could go so far as to exaggerate, let alone invent, the "chatter" that unleashed the jet fighters and the gunboats. Tom Ridge is an honorable man. His soberly cheerful potato face is trustworthiness personified. We all believe him.

Which is what you have to do if you live in a security state. The ordinary citizen is infantilized. Government knows best and its well-brought-up children don't question the parental decisions that are made on their behalf. This compact works (Churchill made it work in Britain during the Second World War) so long as the children don't have reason to believe that their parents are liars, or motivated by mere cupidity—in which case, as in America now, there is a problem. Most of the 46 percent of polled Americans who last week said that they would vote for Howard Dean, in a hypothetical Bush–Dean election in November, believe that the Bush administration has lied its way from Washington to Baghdad and back again, and is out to feather its own nest, Enron- and Halliburton-style. This recalcitrant 46 percent is capable of doubting almost anything asserted by the administration, yet it has no option but to take Tom Ridge and his "chatter" on trust, crossing its fingers that Ridge is as honest as his homely face.

For even the most surly Bush-haters find their doubts checked by the raw fact of September 11, and Americans have grown adept at fashioning their own local versions of catastrophe. Seattle's container port is wedged in a corner of Elliott Bay, right beside the skyscraping (literally so, given our habitual low overcast sky) business district and the football and baseball stadiums. A dirty bomb in a container aboard a ship from Indonesia is the usual scenario. Last May an exercise named TOPOFF 2 put the scenario into rehearsal: actors played the dead and wounded and the emergency services played themselves, with real smoke and flames, overturned buses, and fallen brick and masonry. Drills like this, ever-changing color-coded alerts, surveillance cameras, wiretaps, e-mail hacking, and all the rest of the security paraphernalia keep us reminded, day by day, of the urgent necessity for drills like this, ever-changing color-coded alerts, etc., etc., just as reasons for security must be kept secret because disclosing them would jeopardize security. The whole business is wonderfully, invulnerably circular.

Militant Islamism is no phantom, and there's no shortage of young men who will readily give their lives to emulate Mohamed Atta and inflict a humiliating injury on the hated United States. So we're obliged to believe what we're told—or rather not told—by the Department of Homeland Security. American Civil Liberties Union types and notorious lefties such as Al Gore still persist in querying the terms of the Patriot Act, but only the most rabidly cynical fear that an unprincipled administration, faced with an election, with its leader sliding downward in the polls, could possibly manipulate the outcome by raising the alert to red, filling the skies with fighter planes and the streets with Humvees, to send the citizenry to the polls in a state of suitably chastened insecurity. That couldn't happen in America.

—January 2004

7

HOWARD DEAN

LAST MARCH, I ended a piece for the *Guardian Review* on the line (rather bold, as it seemed at the time) "Watch Howard Dean."[1] Since then, everybody has been watching Dean with increasingly close attention, though nobody yet seems to have his number. He's been plastered with labels—"antiwar," "liberal," "leftist," "angry," "inconsistent," "elitist," and "unelectable." None of these has enough gum on them to stick. The former governor of Vermont describes himself as "an odd duck." He belongs to a species once common throughout the United States, now a rare bird: he is a pragmatic secular rationalist—and the most interesting thing to happen to American politics in a long generation.

From Carter and Reagan to Clinton and George Bush II, a bipartisan religiosity has permeated the language of successive presidential administrations. The present occupant of the White House sees himself as the instrument of God's will, and contenders for his office routinely salute the divinity as if jockeying for His personal campaign endorsement. "Hopes" go hand in hand with "prayers." "Blessings" abound. Abilities are "God-given." This goes far beyond mere churchy pietism. Policy statements are presented as immutable articles of faith.

---

1. See Chapter 4.

To change your mind about, say, school vouchers, or Medicare, or the invasion of Iraq is tantamount to confessing that you no longer believe in Original Sin or the Virgin Birth. "Conviction politics" are theological politics, and in the fundamentalist United States, the believingest country this side of Iran, politicians who adapt their positions to altering circumstances are readily accused of backsliding and apostasy. Like zealous deacons, the American media scans the candidates' political records for "flip-flops"—sure signs of the treacherous apostate.

God is refreshingly absent from Howard Dean's campaign rhetoric. Flip-flops are his natural métier. He is a trimmer by conviction. In Vermont, Dean was tagged as a Rockefeller Republican in Democratic clothing; a frugal, business-friendly budget-balancer. He would infuriate the liberals in his party with his intransigent tight-fistedness on a score of issues, then blindside them by throwing his weight behind a pet liberal project. He was perceived to be governing the state from a position now to the right of the Clinton administration, now to the left of it, but it was moderate Republicans who supplied the votes that won Dean a string of landslide reelections.

When he joined the nomination race, Dean had two planks in his electoral platform: universal health coverage (thanks to him, Vermont now has the most comprehensive program of any state in the nation) and the claim that he could balance the federal budget, as he regularly did in his own state. But that was when he was, as they say, an "asterisk" in the polls, unknown to almost anyone outside Vermont. His position now, as the candidate with the most money, riding a still-building wave of popular support, is largely due to his sustained attack on Bush's handling of the Iraq war.

But Dean is no peacenik. He was all for the invasion of Afghanistan (and, unlike most Democrats, he backed the first Gulf war). As recently as August 2002, when the proposed invasion of Iraq was well in train, he told *The New York Times* that he thought Bush was "doing a fine job on the war on terrorism." By November of that year, he had become a cautious dissident, saying, "We may well end up in a war with Iraq. Saddam Hussein cannot be allowed to possess atomic weapons. But a policy of unbridled unilateralism breeds suspicion at a time when we need the support of our allies around the world." In February 2003 his campaign suddenly took fire when he brought cheering party activists to their feet at the winter meeting of the Democratic National Committee: "What I want to know is ... why in the world the Democratic Party leadership is supporting the President's unilateral attack on Iraq?" In fact this was just one of four "What I want to know is..." questions (the others related to the economy, health care, and education), but the activists barely listened to them, so eager were they to embrace a candidate, any candidate, who would endorse the NO IRAQ WAR stickers on their cars and signs in their yards. Dean then sealed his surprising new identity as the darling of the left by adopting the famous tagline of Paul Wellstone, the liberal senator from Minnesota, who'd died in an air crash just four months before: "I am Howard Dean, and I'm here to represent the democratic wing of the Democratic Party." After the standing ovation that met this announcement, it was easy to miss the rhetorical climax of the text of Dean's speech, which was: "Let me tell you what I want to do for America—and what we've done in Vermont: I want to balance the budget." This went unreported.

Yet Dean's position on the war was inseparable from his stand on the economy: a unilateral (and snooks to Bush's threadbare "coalition of nations") invasion of Iraq was unaffordable in simple budgetary terms, with the federal deficit yawning ever wider as a result of Bush's tax cuts. It was a matter of priorities: improved health care and education, or a war that would drain every last cent, and then some, from the public purse. The speech that gained Dean the passionate support of the American left was at heart the manifesto of a bred-in-the-bone fiscal conservative.

Among the first of the congressional Democrats to endorse Dean was the Seattle congressman Jim McDermott, staunchly of the left, and as temperamentally unakin to Dean, or so I would have thought, as anyone within the very broad church of the Democratic Party. I teased McDermott about his new bedfellow:

> "You know Vermonters call him a Rockefeller Republican?"
> "I want to make love, and I'm not looking for the perfect man. I want to make love to the president again."

Democrats, McDermott said, could not win the presidency if the left deserted them—as it did in the last general election, with a catastrophic defection of liberals from Al Gore to Ralph Nader. So it was important for the left to rally early around an acceptable candidate to forestall another hemorrhage of Democratic voters in 2004.

> "I'm going to give Dean a pass. The left's giving him a pass. If you want Jesus Christ, let's do it in 2008."

The brute facts of the Bush administration, as opposed to its deceptively mild prospect in 2000 (Bush's claim to be "a compassionate conservative," "a uniter not a divider"), have put the left in a uniquely forgiving mood toward Dean. People like McDermott know very well that he isn't one of them, but they love his willingness to tackle Bush head-on. He's "straight," while "this president...if he said it was snowing outside, we'd all go to the window and look." McDermott likens Dean to one of Napoleon's "lucky generals," and nowhere is his luck more apparent than in his effortless hijacking of the ever-troublesome wing of the Democratic Party that lost Gore the last election.

Continuously assailed by his rivals for evasions, contradictions, and misstatements of fact, Dean is successful on the stump and in the town meeting because he has patented a style for communicating the appearance, at least, of straightness and candor. The last election was fought between two hereditary political blue bloods, one of whom was better than the other at conveying the impression that he was just plain folks. The standard of acting set by Dean is altogether higher. His every nuance and gesture says that in his case what you see is what you get. All politicians are actors, but Dean goes to extravagant lengths to act out the part of a man who is not acting.

Bull-necked and stocky, like a cruiserweight boxer, he is rarely seen out of his doctor's dark suit and unfashionably sober necktie. He wears his lineage (a wealthy New York stockbroking family) and education (St. George's School, Newport, where he was a boarder, and Yale University) as if they were no less authentic guarantors of his identity than Senator John Edwards's endless reminders of the fact that he is the son of a millworker (which, on the tenth hearing, begins to sound unnecessarily patronizing to millworkers).

Dean makes it plain that he is not plain folks. He doesn't do hugs, and his handshakes look less than warm. People don't first-name Dean as they did Clinton: even his most gushy supporters refer to him deferentially as "the Gov." He uses patrician words like "contretemps" and "milieu," and peppers his speeches with references to rationalist ancestors like Jefferson, Madison, and Thomas Paine. Where Clinton, at this stage of the 1992 primaries, introduced a program named, preachily, "the New Covenant," Dean has introduced a similar program called "the New Social Contract" (goodbye, First Baptist Church; hello, Hobbes and Rousseau). The personal questions that have had other candidates tying themselves up in verbal knots have been briskly dispatched by Dean: yes, he smoked pot (who didn't?); yes, he drank heavily when he was a student ("I used to get hammered at weekends and it was really bad for me," he told a class of Vermont high schoolers); no, he didn't want to go to Vietnam (he escaped the draft with a doctor's letter and an X-ray photo of his spine, then spent the best part of a year skiing in Vail).

When Gore endorsed Howard Dean on December 9, first in Harlem, then in Cedar Rapids, Iowa, the contrasting styles of the two politicians could hardly have been made more plain. Gore spoke as if he were in church, in his down-home "Tennessee" voice, pulling every vowel out into a tortured diphthong, sawing the air with his right hand, and packing every slow sentence with heavy emphases. "...[Dean] speaks from the heart, and he doesn't hold back, and he tries to say and do what's right for this country, and I like that!" He seemed to be not so much endorsing Dean as giving him a born-again testimony. I found Gore painful to listen to: I wanted to tell him I wasn't deaf, wasn't in first-grade Sunday school, and that this was exactly the sort of faux-folksy performance that turned off so many voters in the 2000 election.

As usual, Dean talked a mile a minute, in rapid, rippling, pyrrhic lines whose only stress fell on the last or penultimate syllable. There's an impatient rasp in his voice; he always appears to have far more to say than time will allow. His sentences are crowded with facts, figures, and opinions, delivered in a studiedly neutral tone as if he were rattling off a string of self-explanatory syllogisms. "Angry" is the wrong word for Dean, though he is adept at tapping the anger of others, and is apt to bristle irritably when challenged. On the platform, he is cool to the point of being emotionless—a manner he relieves with wintry humor. His curtailed smiles are quick as eyeblinks. When he tells a town meeting, as he nearly always does, that "we're going to have a little fun at the President's expense tonight," he makes clear that the impending fun is going to be of a very dour variety.

Dean presents himself as a postmodern, post-ideological politician. Central to this is his calculated rejection of high-flown religious language in favor of the vocabulary and grammar of worldly common sense. What both excites his admirers and irritates his detractors is that they've never heard a candidate for the presidency talking like this before. Joe Lieberman (who finishes every speech with a presumptuous

"God bless you") has insinuated that Dean is too irreligious for America. "Some people," Lieberman said, meaning Dean, "believe that faith has no place in the so-called public square.... Some people forget that faith was central to our founding and remains central to our national purpose and our individual lives."

Faith, together with its near synonyms in American politics, vision and dream, is a code word for down-the-line ideological consistency, for a value system that can be expressed as a ten-point creed. Dean's "odd-duck" positions—on gun control, retirement age, the death penalty, Social Security and Medicare, the environment, same-sex civil unions, and much more—suggest a frank regard for expediency of a kind that's often practiced but never preached. The nearest he comes to voicing an inflexible article of faith is his Polonius-like insistence that budgets can and must be balanced.

When pressed, as *The Boston Globe* pressed him in a Christmas Eve interview, Dean says he is a Congregationalist (his wife and children are nonpracticing Jews) who greatly admires the "example" of Jesus Christ while declining to discuss any supernatural beliefs he may hold. He promises to talk more about his religion when his campaign travels to the South—an expedient move if ever there was one.

He has infuriated both his Democratic rivals and many members of the press corps, who have been reduced to tallying his "flip-flops" and reading his remarks as if they were the entrails of a peculiarly ominous goat. In his February speech to the Democratic National Committee, he drew widespread applause when he said the party must recover the votes of Reagan Democrats, whom he characterized, deftly, as "white folks in the South who drive pickup trucks with Confederate flag decals on the back." In November, this line was solemnly exhumed (by the Democratic rivals) as evidence that Dean was insensitive to black feelings. When he remarked that the arrest of Saddam Hussein had not made America safer, he was reviled on all sides as "impolitic," "unpatriotic," "ludicrous," and "unhinged."

The critics had to pipe down six days later, when the head of Home-land Security, Tom Ridge, raised the alert from yellow to orange, say-ing that the threat of terrorist attack on the United States was "greater now than at any point since September 11, 2001"—Dean's point exactly.

It's becoming a law of this political season that whenever Dean makes what the news media perceives as a fatal misstep, another flood of small donations (about $75 is the average) pours into his campaign. In June 2003, his appearance on *Meet the Press* with Tim Russert was generally reviewed as "disastrous." Dean equivocated. He gave com-plex answers to yes/no questions. He betrayed impatience with the tone of his interviewer (Russert is notably deferential to members of the Re-publican establishment; with Dean, he exhibited a hitherto unsus-pected potential as an attack dog). All this went down very badly with the columnists and commentators, but very well with viewers at home: that Sunday, DeanforAmerica.com chalked up its best-ever fund-raising day. Most people don't much like either journalists or politicians: Dean appears to share their feeling for journalists, and has a greatly underrated knack of not looking and sounding like a politician.

In fact he is at least as politically experienced, crafty, and ambi-tious as Clinton (another five-term governor) was in 1992. But where Clinton, when cornered, used to fall back on his ineffable brand of legalistic sophistry ("It all depends on what the meaning of the word 'is' is") and thereby alienate even his own supporters, Dean acts the part of the brusque doctor, summoned from his country surgery to attend a grave case of dementia in Washington, D. C., and mops up votes with even his most "impolitic" performances. Doctors—unlike lawyers, journalists, and politicians—are popular figures, and Dean's time as a physician (he was in private practice in Vermont from 1981 to 1991) shapes his whole political rhetoric. Answering questions at town meetings, which is something he excels at, he rattles dispassion-ately through the diagnosis, talking, as doctors do, a little above the patient's head; then he prescribes the treatment, in language comprehensible to a child. I've seen audience after audience succumb gratefully to Dean's air of superior professional authority. No other candidate for the nomination comes close to matching him in this.

With his doctor-patient manners, Dean is very much a top-down politician. But his campaign, run by Joe Trippi, is a novel and audacious exercise in bottom-up politics. Dean, who looks happiest when he has several cubic yards of body space to separate him from other people, is cool; the necessary fuzziness and warmth are supplied by the campaign, by Trippi's "online populism" at DeanforAmerica.com. The Web site, besides being a $10,000-an-hour moneymaking machine, is an exceptionally lively virtual community—a beguiling combination of noisy chat rooms, agitprop updated for the Internet era, and a networking-and-dating service. Skip the continuously changing official blog, and the unofficial bloggers who hang out morning, noon, and night in the forums, and go to DeanLink, where you can plug in your zip code and find every self-styled "Deaniac" in your immediate neighborhood. Some post their personal biographies, along with lonely-hearts-style snapshots. Click on a name, and up come two buttons: "Send a message to ——" and "Add —— to your list of friends." It's hard to remember that this is politics, not the dating game. Then go to "Get Local," where the virtual spills into the actual, and you can meet up with —— in the flesh at a fund-raising house party, a letter-writing and envelope-licking session at a bar or café, a doorbelling expedition, a chilly hour spent waving Dean placards at the passing traffic. You can still sign up to travel to Iowa to get out the vote for the caucus there on Monday, or to New Hampshire for the primary a week later on Tuesday. For anyone who happens not to have a life, a busy, socially crowded, full-time one awaits at DeanforAmerica.com.

Trippi describes the campaign with a software metaphor: it is "open source" rather than "proprietary," Linux as against Microsoft, in which the individual user is free to adapt the campaign's considerable resources to his or her own personal and local circumstances. It is, so the Web site relentlessly iterates, "Your campaign," shaped and driven by its nationwide community of members. Even the casual visitor is liable to get infected by the air of urgency and excitement that pervades the site. In America's present sullen climate, it's an unseasonably warm and hopeful place to go.

Huge claims are being made for Dean's online campaign—that it is changing the character of American democracy, reclaiming for the electoral process a great mass of young voters, and is, as Trippi says, "the greatest grassroots campaign in history."

Maybe. But the actual figures suggest otherwise. Between the end of June and the end of September, Americans for Dean grew steadily at the rate of just under 4,000 new members a day, from 100,000 to 450,000. Given the press and TV attention paid to Dean since September, one might have expected to see an accelerating upward curve in membership, taking the numbers to somewhere between one million and two million by the end of the year, well in line with the great equation of Trippi's $100 Revolution: "two million Americans x $100 = George W. Bush Out of Office." In fact, there has been no curve, but a shallowing line; people have joined the campaign at a rate of only 1,100 a day in the last quarter, bringing the total membership to just over 550,000 at year's end. What this might suggest is that the idea of "community" is subject to a natural size limit. In July, when there were 200,000 Americans for Dean, spread coast to coast across the country, joining the club may have been seen as an intimate avowal of like-mindedness. Is the club losing its cachet now that Dean is the front-runner and a household name? Is the core of Dean supporters getting hollowed out? Or will the primaries and Dean's likely nomination bring the vital surge in membership that Trippi anticipated in September?

Whatever happens, the campaign is still a new kind of engine in American politics—easy on fuel at $75 a pop, instantly responsive in emergencies (as when a sudden influx of money is needed to counter an attack on the candidate), and with greater reserves of human power under its hood than any Democrat has been able to call on in the past. The question of just what this beast can do when driven flat-out is clearly beginning to trouble the Republicans as they watch it cruise easily past Kerry, Lieberman, and the rest (Dean is currently neck and neck with Dick Gephardt in the Iowa polls, and the barely tested candidacy of the retired general Wesley Clark, whose platform largely consists of his old campaign medals, is now the most unpredictable element in the nomination race).

Dean isn't unelectable. To win in the primaries, he needs the support of the left (always a tough constituency for him). He has now captured the left with his stand on Iraq, leaving the one true leftist, Dennis Kucinich, in the dust, and has already moved on to his original main agenda—health insurance, education, and the economy. These were the issues that kept on winning him Republican votes in Vermont, where he was so well liked by the right that Republicans ran a succession of weak candidates against him to ensure his survival as governor. He's not, as some have said, a centrist, let alone a "closet centrist": he's all over the place; right, left, center, and every point between. He is a consistent pragmatist and meliorist who has spent his political life tinkering with the status quo, and leaving it generally somewhat improved by his efforts. Just before Christmas, he nicely defined his approach when talking to a group of New Hampshire doctors about his plan for national health coverage: "This is not a perfect plan. This is a plan designed to pass." Passable imperfection— Dean's hallmark as a politician—has never looked more attractive than it does now.

America has lately endured a surfeit of perfect plans, including Bush's economic growth and tax relief reconciliation act of 2001, which has brought about the gigantic and still-mounting federal deficit, along with the strange, jobless economic "recovery," and Paul

Wolfowitz's brilliant scheme for democratizing the Middle East at no cost to the American taxpayer (Iraqi oil was going to amply pay for both the invasion and reconstruction).

The mind of the ideologue is continually buzzing with perfect plans; only the realist understands the value of imperfect ones, and Dean, alone among the Democratic candidates, is tapping into the mood of chastened realism that has settled on the country during the last two and a half years. He alone is deploying the rhetoric of corrosive common sense to expose the evasions, contradictions, and flights of wishful thinking in the language of the Bush administration. Watching him on television as he roused a socially mixed audience in Ames, Iowa, with a particularly well-delivered variant of his standard stump speech, moving from a leisurely low-key discussion of bovine spongiform encephalopathy (imagine Bush pronouncing that) and into a blistering deconstruction of administration policies, one could feel the excitement building in the hall as he translated inarticulate discontent into cold numbers, reasons, arguments, diagnoses, and medications. No one else is doing this with anything like Dean's stylistic dazzle and assurance.

Dean—assuming he wins the nomination—can be counted on to hang on to the disaffected liberals who voted for Nader last time around, and to attract a sizeable chunk of the 49 percent of the electorate who didn't bother to show up at the polls. The interesting question is how he will play with the Bush voters of 2000, and here his secularism becomes an issue, and not necessarily to his disadvantage.

Many votes in 2000 did not so much go to Bush as drift capriciously on the breeze into his camp. In those flush times the Lewinsky affair was reason enough not to vote Democrat. Gore bored. Bush was a fresh face. He promised to "reach out across the partisan divide," to "build consensus" in "a new spirit of cooperation" and "end the bitterness and wrangling in Washington." He promised to "stop extending our troops all around the world in nation-building exercises." He sounded amiably, reassuringly harmless.

The floating voters who floated idly his way—and they were legion—liked the sound of Bush because he appeared at the time to be ideology-free. They were certainly not signing up for membership in the hard Christian right, and weren't expecting to be drafted into a ceaseless, unendable war between the Forces of Good and the Axis of Evil. In 2000 the constitutional separation of church and state was a conversational topic of distinctly limited interest. But in 2004 church and state have become so deeply entwined that religious doctrine dictates policy and policy is preached as religious doctrine. Even steadfast believers are wondering if the spirit of Luke 20:25 is being dangerously broached.

Dean famously gave up membership of the Episcopalian Church and became a Congregationalist because the Episcopalians were being uncooperative about a proposed bike path that led across their property. One moral of the story is that large shifts of cultural and philosophical allegiance tend to get triggered by mundane disgruntlements, and Dean has a wickedly sure grasp of the value of the mundane: he talks about money—paychecks, taxes, health insurance costs, school funding—so vividly that you can hear the rustle of the bills, bringing the big numbers of economics down to palpable sums that you might find in your own pocket.

Although President Bush does well in the patriotism and godliness department, he has little grasp of the kind of bike-path issues on which Dean is reliably eloquent. Standing alone at a rostrum without his advisers, Bush is eminently beatable in debate. As the former treasury secretary, Paul O'Neill, revealed this week, the President is clueless about economics—Dean's strongest suit.

Dean promises to wrest American government from the ideologues and refocus it on sublunary matters like hospitals, and schools, and the affordability of war. He has positioned himself as the candidate of fact versus theory, empiricism versus idealism. Pace Joe Lieberman, the United States was founded not by Pilgrim Fathers but by eighteenth-century rationalists, and Dean speaks out of a tradition more impeccably American than that of the soi-disant men of faith who occupy the Bush White House.

He is squarely buttressed by James Madison, who wrote that "religion and government will both exist in greater purity the less they are mixed together," and "theories are the offspring of the closet; exceptions and qualifications are the lessons of experience." Because he's the first presidential candidate in living memory to try to represent that tradition, Dean is still viewed as a suspicious novelty, liable to implode at any moment. But if he survives the primaries and gets the nomination, it's easy to imagine him rousing the national electorate as he now rouses grassroots Democrats in the Northeast and beyond (a crowd of eight thousand turned out to listen to him speak here in Seattle).

At the very least, he is sketching a believable picture of how America might be if Bush were not its president, which in these illiberal days is a rare tonic in itself.

—January 2004

8

EMASCULATING ARABIA

SEEING THE TERRIBLE pictures of the beheading of Nicholas Berg, it's easy to miss the significance of the soundtrack that accompanies them. The taped voice—presumably that of Abu Musab al-Zarqawi, the Jordanian associate of Osama bin Laden—rails not so much against the Bush administration as against the torpor of the Arab world:

> The shameful photos are evil humiliation for Muslim men and women in the Abu Ghraib prison. Where is the sense of honor, where is the rage? Where is the anger for God's religion? Where is the sense of veneration for Muslims, and where is the sense of vengeance for the honor of Muslim men and women in the crusaders' prisons?

Professing himself to be outraged by the absence of Arab outrage at the photos from Abu Ghraib, al-Zarqawi proceeds with his gruesome remake of the videotaped killing of Daniel Pearl in Pakistan in 2002.

That portion of al-Zarqawi's repellent message—his claim that people in the Middle East haven't been as shocked by the Abu Ghraib pictures as one might expect—is surely true. For days, there was a feeling of tentative, nervous relief in the United States that the pictures streaming out of Abu Ghraib had not—yet—provoked the wave of uncontrollable and violent popular protest across the Arab world that many Americans had feared. It was suggested that Arabs are so inured to torture in their own countries that they have lost the ability to be shocked by it, and also that Iraqi Shia Muslims and Kurds were unlikely to be greatly upset by the sight of Baathist Sunnis getting a taste of their own medicine from their Western jailers.

Both of these quasi explanations were self-serving shots in the dark. What was clear from reading the English-language Arab press over last weekend was the truth of the old saying: "American viciously humiliates Arab" is not news; only when the terms are reversed are headlines made. To most of the Arab editorial writers, and perhaps to most Arabs, the digital photos merely confirmed what they had been saying since long before the invasion of Iraq took place: America is on an Orientalist rampage in which Arabs are systematically denatured, dehumanized, stripped of all human complexity, reduced to naked babyhood.

Defining the Orientalist project, Edward Said wrote of how Occidentals feminized and infantilized Arabs, crediting them with "feminine" traits like intuition and an incapacity for reason (so Arab magicians figure large in the mythology, but Arab mathematicians not at all), and rendered Arabia as pliant, sensuous, passive, awaiting penetration by the rational masculine West.

In classic Orientalist fashion, Iraq was brutally simplified before it was invaded. Because of the way that the British, operating on the principle of divide and rule, had cobbled together three profoundly dissimilar Ottoman provinces to make a nation, Iraq stands alone in the Arab world in its complex rifts of religion, politics, tribe, race, and class. For eighty years, Iraq has been an immensely tricky spiderweb of social and cultural lines and intersections. None of this was recognized by the invaders. As recently as last January, so we are told, George Bush was cheerfully ignorant of the deepest, most conspicuous fault line in Iraqi society: the division between Sunni and Shia.

The Bush administration rhetorically homogenized the several peoples of Iraq by endless iteration of the phrase "the Iraqi people," or, when speaking of Saddam, "his own people."

When Saddam's gang of Tikritis gassed Kurdish villages or drained the water from the Marsh Arabs' swamps, they were decidedly not dealing with their "own people" but with people they regarded as dangerous aliens: tribally, racially, religiously, politically distinct from themselves. Now, when coalition forces insist on blaming "foreign fighters" for homegrown Iraqi insurrections, they unconsciously mirror the mind-set of the Baathists, who regarded Kurds and southern Shias as equally foreign fighters. War, said Ambrose Bierce, is God's way of teaching Americans geography, and in the last year some human geography has been learned, mainly to the effect that a large number of Iraqi people appear not to belong to the Iraqi people—that Orientalist construct which was the catchphrase of 2002.

The Iraqi people were pictured as yearning, femininely, childishly, with one voice, for a pluralist free-market democracy, and (bad taste though it is to recall this detail) they would greet their liberators, femininely, childishly, with flowers. In the early autumn of 2002, the secretary-general of the Arab League, Amr Moussa, warned that a Western invasion of Iraq would "open the gates of hell," but the Orientalists listened to no one from the region, preferring to trust the Middle Eastern expertise of Paul Wolfowitz, who blithely represented Iraq as a comely bride, trapped in a dungeon by her wicked stepfather.

By the time of the invasion, Iraq had been so exhaustively Orientalized that it had lost almost all connection to reality. Much of this effort was grandly sentimental, oozing goodwill toward "the Iraqi people." All of it was dehumanizing, robbing Iraqis of their intractable particularity. None of it fooled the long-memoried Arabs in neighboring states, who had seen this stuff many times before, and who might, perhaps, have recognized in the perorations of Wolfowitz of Arabia the ghostly voice of T. E. Lawrence in the poem that prefaces

Seven Pillars of Wisdom with a breathtakingly vain promise of mutual orgasm:

> *I loved you, so I drew these tides of men into my hands*
> *and wrote my will across the sky in stars*
> *To earn you Freedom, the seven-pillared worthy house,*
> *that your eyes might be shining for me*
> *When we came.*

In the event, Lawrence's seed was spilled, like Onan's, and like that of every Orientalist who has dreamed of liberating Arabia, on the sand.

It is necessary to go over this old and painful ground in order to read the messages from Abu Ghraib. One searches the photos in vain for signs of furtiveness on the part of the torturers, for any indication that they were snapped on the sly. To the contrary: the soldiers, fresh-faced, smiling, happy, look as if they are taking pride in a job well done—and the job in question looks like the Orientalist enterprise, acted out in gross cartoon form. Here is Arabia nude, faceless under a hood, or ridiculously feminized in women's panties, forced into infantile masturbatory sex and sodomy. (These people are ruled by their nether organs, not by their higher faculties, is the Orientalist line.) The jail has become a grotesque nursery, with Private Lynndie England (her very name like the nom de guerre of a sex worker), cigarette jutting from her cheerful grin, playing the part of the au pair from hell. The pictures appear to be so single-minded in their intent, so artfully directed, so relentlessly Orientalist in their conception, that one looks instinctively for a choreographer—a senior intelligence officer, perhaps, who keeps Edward Said on his bedside table, and ransacks the book each night for new ideas.

That speculation is probably misplaced. A chilling story in last Saturday's *New York Times* made plain that the humiliations depicted in the Abu Ghraib pictures are regularly practiced in domestic American prisons. The reporter, Fox Butterfield, dug up examples of hooding, stripping naked, and forced sex inflicted by guards in jails in Arizona, Utah, Virginia, and Texas. At least two of the American soldiers due to be court-martialed are reservists who are "corrections officers" in civilian life, and it seems likely that in Baghdad they were indulging in sadistic amusements perfected back home in the US. Dehumanization is an international language with a universal grammar, and Orientalism is one of its local dialects—a distinction that will, unfortunately, be lost on every Arab and Muslim who brings the photos up on his or her computer.

However fortuitously, the pictures of torture fit snugly into the larger pattern of the Orientalist conquest of Arabia as it is perceived on the peninsula. What began as romantic simplification of the real life of Iraq—the Wolfowitz scenario—culminates in the erasure of human identity and the rendering of men and women as inanimate objects.

Seymour Hersh, who broke the Abu Ghraib story in *The New Yorker*, quotes Specialist Matthew Wisdom of the Military Police: "I remember ssg Frederick hitting one prisoner in the side of its ribcage.... I saw two naked detainees, one masturbating to another with its mouth open." When pronouns drift so casually from he to it (and the speaker here is a whistle-blower, not a torturer), we are in a nightmare world where men are barely distinguishable from flies or black beetles.

The gruesome murder of Nicholas Berg should not obscure the fact that the pictures from Abu Ghraib were generally accepted in the Muslim world with eerie, almost philosophical calm. It is as if they knew all along that it was like this. Even before President Bush drew tides of men into his hands and wrote his will across the sky in stars, and long before the goons with digital cameras came on the scene, Arabs knew they were thought of as "it"s.

A released detainee, quoted by *The New York Times* on May 10, says: "I realized [the Americans] came to obliterate a whole society, a whole civilization"—a thought so old and so commonplace that one might hear it uttered, world-wearily, in any Arab café anywhere across the globe. The questionable truth of the thought hardly matters now: it is so widely believed, so amply, extravagantly confirmed in the grinning face of Lynndie England. "American humiliates Arab" is not news. Unfortunately for us, those—like al-Zarqawi's al-Qaeda franchise—bent on exploiting the injuries of the humiliated know all too well what does make news.

—May 2004

9

TERMINA CAMINO RURAL

MY ELEVEN-YEAR-OLD DAUGHTER, Julia, had been taking Spanish classes at school, and wanted to try out her fledgling linguistic skills in Mexico. I saw the opportunity for an extended lesson in West Coast history and geography. So we spent Julia's spring break driving 1,650 miles from Seattle to Baja California, our destination a speck of a fishing village, not marked on most maps, on Baja's Pacific coast. The great American road trip is an ailing form: American children now tend to measure the distances of their enormous country in terms of how many inflight movies it takes to get from A to B or Z. I meant to be a purist. We'd shun interstate freeways wherever humanly possible, we'd drop the top of my two-seater convertible and open ourselves to the smell of the land, and we'd talk all the way. In my experience, the best parent–child conversations happen in the car, when you're both facing ahead and confidences can be exchanged without meeting each other's eyes.

We left Seattle before dawn on Easter Thursday, just as Condoleezza Rice was beginning to give evidence to the 9/11 Commission in Washington, D. C. Her voice disappeared in crackle soon after we left the freeway and struck west across the Olympic Peninsula on a road striped with the long shadows of Douglas firs. Moments after turning off the radio, we slowed past the huddled remains of a black bear on the roadside. This was Julia's first sighting of a bear in the wild, and she mourned its death to the point of—uncharacteristic—tears. She did not see, and I did not point out to her, the roadkill coyote, quickly followed by a roadkill deer. Washington State that morning was littered with large dead mammals who'd collided with trucks the night before, their bodies sprawled in sunshine at the feet of the black firs.

Breakfasting at the Rusty Tractor restaurant, over maps and notebooks, full of our trip, Julia's mood perked up no end at the sight of three men sitting at the bar, all wearing plaid lumberjack shirts and all smoking pipes. "It's like a sitcom," she said. Only ninety minutes out of Seattle, we were already in that other world, so close to fiction in its appearance of exotic simplicity, after which every tourist hankers.

Because the major geological fault lines of America run roughly north to south, a coast-to-coast journey is punctuated—at long, often painfully long intervals—by unforgettable geographic events: the Cascades, the Continental Divide in the Rocky Mountains, the Great Plains, the Mississippi, the Appalachians. Going north to south, what mainly changes is the climate. Between western Washington and Baja you travel from wet to dry, from a sopping 120 inches of rainfall a year to a parched half-dozen or less. So at 60 mph, you're losing annual rainfall at an average rate of about five inches an hour, with the speeding landscape altering subtly around you as thirsty firs give way to pines, then redwoods, then deciduous live oaks, then palms, until you reach the arid southern latitudes of cactus, agave, and sage.

At 10 AM we crossed from Washington to Oregon on the low three-mile bridge over the Columbia River estuary, where the Lewis and Clark expedition arrived, in vile weather, in November 1805. Clark's journal describes the "tremendious wind" and "emence waves & Swells" encountered by their canoes. For us, the sky was blue, the water like tinfoil, its surface scrolled with arabesques of tide and current. Ignoring the city of Astoria on the Oregon shore, we kept on running south on the coast road as it wormed its way over wooded cliffs, with the Pacific foaming like milk around the rocky headlands and the air thick with the tang of salt and pine. This spirit-lifting ride was punctuated at too-regular intervals by small, banal resort towns, each a carbon copy of the last: same gas station, same Burger King, same gift shop, same tackle store, same overblown motel. At Seaside, Julia put on her new sunglasses, and I saw us reflected in the unfriendly stares of curious pedestrians—we looked uncannily like Humbert Humbert and Lolita. I wanted to call out, "She's my daughter, I'm her dad," but remembered that was Humbert's line too.

The road took a brief eastward swing inland, through flat dairy-farming country and the—to me—English country-holiday smell of sundried cowpats. We passed the factory that makes Julia's preferred brand of cheese and returned to the rim of the sea. A quick break for lunch at Lincoln Beach, and we were off again, haring through once-prosperous timber and fishing ports, now down on their luck and trying, with very mixed success, to recreate themselves as vacation and retirement communities: Newport, Florence, Reedsport, North Bend, Coos Bay.

Cliffs petered out into sand dunes and cranberry bogs. Julia slotted in a tape of Dick Cavett reading—utterly engagingly—from a horribly edited version of *Huckleberry Finn*.

Half drifting down the Mississippi, half racing through Oregon, I thought of the odd couples in American mythology—Huck and Jim, Lewis and Clark, Ishmael and Queequeg. Paul Bunyan had his blue ox, Babe. Thelma had Louise. Humbert had Lolita. Classic American wanderers go in twosomes across the land, where European ones, from Ulysses to Wilfred Thesiger, travel most typically alone. This is the sort of partially baked notion that's liable to come to mind as you bite into the fifth hundred-mile chunk of the day.

With 476 miles on the tripometer and about fifty miles to go before the California state line, we stopped at Port Orford and checked into an amiably scruffy motel. Filling in the guest form, I was aware of the eyes of the motherly lady owner moving swiftly, surreptitiously, from Julia to me and back again. But we evidently passed the test, for she immediately began to talk about dogs to Julia and to warn me of the "spendy" restaurant up the street, which I took—correctly, as it turned out—as a useful recommendation.

Port Orford was a queer kind of port. In the cheap bar of the spendy restaurant, I was told that the US Corps of Engineers had built a breakwater so ineffectual that any boat taking overnight shelter behind it was likely to be smashed to matchwood on the rocks. So the entire fleet of thirty or so substantial crab and rockfish boats had to be lifted in and out of the water every day with a pair of hydraulic cranes. In the quiet of the night, listening to the ocean boil and growl around the open cove, I thought that only in can-do, nature-conquering America would anyone think of maintaining a fishing fleet in such an inhospitable place. Yet I see that in 2000 well over a million pounds of fish were landed here, which must say something about the stubborn, never-take-no-for-an-answer character of Port Orfordians.

We were up at 5:30 and on the road before 6:00. Black cliffs, black trees, black sea, and the surf breaking silver on the rocks—like driving inside a daguerreotype. Julia, groaning faintly, went back to sleep in the passenger seat, waking just in time to take a snap of the Welcome to California sign in chilly, thin sea fog.

"Which American president, elected with the slimmest majority in history, immediately took the country on an imperial war against a nation rich in mineral assets?"

Julia, on conversational autopilot, said, "George W. Bush."

Actually it was the eleventh president, not the forty-third. On a doubtful pretext, James K. Polk went to war against Mexico from 1846 to 1848, winning nearly three quarters of a million square miles of territory for the US—Texas, Arizona, New Mexico, Nevada,

Colorado, Utah, Wyoming, and California—and thereby fulfilled the great catchphrase of the 1840s, that it was America's "manifest destiny" to stretch from coast to coast, from the Gulf Stream waters to the redwood forests. A thousand miles north of the present border, we were already in what used to be Mexico before the Invasión Yanqui.

California had been a pushover then, with only about six thousand white inhabitants, most connected with the string of coastal missions, each as big as a small town, that stretched from San Francisco through Baja along the Camino Real. The missions were largely the work of an eighteenth-century Franciscan priest from Mallorca, Junipero Serra—short, fat, given to extravagant and bloody self-flagellation—who tyrannized the Indians under his rule while saving their immortal souls. It seemed appropriate on Good Friday morning to remember that the state now known to all the world as the capital of hedonism was once a severe Catholic hierocracy.

The redwoods began almost as soon as the state line was crossed—mostly hundred-year-old youngsters planted between the gigantic rotting stumps of felled trees ten and twenty times that age. Past the dull city of Eureka, the road bent away from the ocean and wound and swooped through the forested mountains of Humboldt County—a fast and brilliant ride that felt like flying. We stopped to eat at a Hansel and Gretel–like clearing in the forest named Phillipsville, and sped on down through live oaks, horse farms, vineyards, and ominous, stifling heat. At Willits, in Mendocino County, where we pulled over for a drink in an air-conditioned café, it was 90 Fahrenheit in the shade.

The woman who served Julia an iced soda and me a local chardonnay said, "It was never like this at this time of year. These hot spells started just a couple of years ago: now we're getting used to it." She promised us coolth in San Francisco, where Julia had set her heart on spending the night. When we got back to the car, whose top I had foolishly left open, the seats were hot as griddles. Julia yelped as she sat down.

One could feel the magnetic pull of the Bay Area cities from 150 miles away, as traffic thickened in the standing heat, and by Santa Rosa we were moving at a painful crawl, the air violet with exhaust fumes and angry with morosely fuming drivers. Route 101 looked like a greenhouse gasworks. Julia was lost to a tape of *Treasure Island* on the stereo system.

The Golden Gate Bridge had been near the top of her list of attractions on the trip south. In the event, only the uppermost part of the rust-red southern tower protruded above a roiling, sunlit bank of fog. We rumbled across, nose-to-tail, with visibility down to about twenty feet.

"It's not fair," Julia said.

"It may be a sign of climate change," I said. For this fog was summer fog, sucked in from the sea by the baking hinterland, and eerily early for Easter. Feeling our way though the murk, we talked about how carbon dioxide lets light in but won't let heat out—a subject on which Julia, who had an ace fifth-grade science teacher named Doc O, was better informed than me.

"Look—Polk Street," she said, as we headed for the tacky grid of streets around Fishermen's Wharf, where we found a room for the night with a view (if you craned your head far enough around the edge of the balcony) of Alcatraz. Flaky from the day's driving, I was taken by Julia on a ride to nowhere in a yellow streetcar, refused point-blank to enter the wax museum, and walked far enough out on a pier to make sure the fog hadn't lifted over Golden Gate. It was Julia who found us the cool, quiet haven of an oak-timbered Italian restaurant, where I cured my headache with Barolo and saltimbocca.

By dawn on Saturday, the fog had taken possession of the downtown streets: the coast road would be viewless. So we ran south through the low-rise white-box architecture of Silicon Valley, past the campus of Stanford University, the nursery of the billionaire child-graduates who engineered the digital revolution, to the sprawl of San José, in welcome sunshine. With Julia now an expert map reader, we struck out for Carmel on the coast.

"Route 101 turns into 156 in about four miles. Then we want 1 to Monterey." This was a new skill, picked up in the last couple of days, and I was properly thankful for it; surprised, too, for Julia had never before shown any interest in the maps, charts, atlases, and globes that collect around me in my part of the house. From San Francisco to Baja, I left the business of navigation to her.

The twisty, up-hill, down-dale road over the cliffs from Carmel to San Luis Obispo is said to be one of the most spectacular drives in the United States. But the fog was back that morning, and apart from a freakish sunbreak over Big Sur, the view was of pebbly gray tarmac fading into nothingness a few yards ahead. We made up the surrounding landscape as we went along—surf, crags, beaches, coves, palaces, new glories emerging with every fresh corkscrew turn. For 130 miles we plowed through this nebulous and speculative world, peopling it, unpeopling it, fiddling like gods with its probable geology, until at last the sun broke through in earnest on the disappointing reality of Morro Bay.

But San Luis Obispo, a few miles on, was not disappointing.

"It looks like Mexico," Julia said, admiring its wealth of faux pink adobe. The city looked like a toddler's birthday cake, elaborately tunneled by mice. Father Junipero Serra's godly activities along the coast had inspired a riot of Victorian "mission-style" architecture in California and the Southwest, and San Luis Obispo consisted of almost nothing else. We parked the car in the shade of a palm tree, and ate an extravagant lunch in a building whimsically reminiscent of an old Spanish church. In the floor-to-ceiling mirror by our table, I saw how we looked: two whey-faced tourists from the far north among the permanent tans of Southern Californians.

Santa Barbara, 120 miles south (120 miles had come to seem no more than a lick and a spit), was the home of our friend Trish

Reynales, whose hard-to-find house was somewhere up among the small canyons, where the town backed onto the Santa Barbara mountains to the north. Working from my scribbled directions, we drove slowly through jasmine-smelling streets of high-walled gardens bursting with spring greenery: palms, yuccas, oaks, agaves like giant artichokes, bougainvillea. In every driveway, a Porsche or a Mercedes, and in some a Porsche and a Mercedes. Yet in dry Southern California, wealth is most eloquently expressed in terms of water consumption, and the walled gardens, like miniature tropical rain forests, were a truer measure of Santa Barbara's riches than its expensive cars.

After some wrangles and wrong turnings, we found Trish's place: a small, elegant, angular, airy house, designed as a painter's studio and built on the lip of a seasonal creek. Her garden, too, was lavishly green and full of flowers. Buried sprinklers popped up to the orders of a digital box on the wall by the front door—a device as crucial to the culture of Southern California as the elevator is to life in Manhattan.

For like LA, Santa Barbara is an artificial oasis, watered from afar by an ingenious system of pipes, tunnels, dams, aqueducts. Left to itself, it would be sagebrush and cactus, but American capital and hydroengineering wizardry have made it greener than wet Seattle. Cooled by the ocean and the frigid California current, moistened with computer-controlled imported water, it's the sort of place that, once set foot in, immediately inspires dreams of moving there. "I'd like to live in Santa Barbara," Julia said—as who wouldn't?

In the neighborhood Italian restaurant that evening, Kirk Douglas, looking frail but vital, was seated at the next table. Following the Santa Barbara social code, we strenuously pretended not to have noticed.

Next morning, Mexico-bound at last, we tiptoed through the house in the dark, trying not to wake our hostess. The quarter-moon was still bright in the sky as we sped past the lines of paling surf on the beaches. On a weekday at this time Route 101 would be a parking lot, but everyone was sleeping in on Easter Sunday and the road was almost empty. In that gray and muggy twilight that usually precedes intense heat, I fed the car into the delirious tangle of Los Angeles freeways, with Julia calling out instructions at my side.

Following the example of the locals, we hurtled from freeway to freeway at a steady eighty-five, collapsing the epic city into a space considerably shorter in time than that of the average English snarled-up market town, until, speed-shocked and jittery, I took the Long Beach exit and we emerged on the sedate and pretty Pacific Coast Highway that leads to San Clemente. How civilized the stoplights seemed—each allowing a pause to take in the ocean.

Julia said, "What exactly does that pedal on the left do?" I explained the clutch. She went on to quiz me about the lights, signals, windshield wipers, and the cruise control I've never dared to use.

"What's this about?" I asked.

"I've been thinking. I'm going to have to learn to drive. I'd really like to do this drive again, when I'm, like, twenty-two."

"That's a strangely Los Angelean thought. How long have you been thinking it?"

"All morning. I've got it figured out. What I'd really like is a convertible green Bug. Or maybe silver. Or blue."

At San Clemente we joined the automotive hell of Interstate 5, sandwiched between eighteen-wheelers whose drivers appeared to have forgotten it was Easter Day and they should have been at church. I prayed that the Catholic truck drivers of Mexico would have better memories. From the suburbs of San Diego, Tijuana appeared in the distance as a hilly, blue industrial haze.

"Mexico!" Julia said, as one might say "Samarkand!"

It was 11 AM, and we still had far to go. Driving through Tijuana, I saw Los Angeles again, same sprawl, same hills, but tan, not green; a threadbare Los Angeles, perilously short of money, and what money buys in the far West, water. Looking up to the Tijuana version of

Beverly Hills, one could see not millionaire mansions but untidy encampments of squatters' shacks. At the Mexican border, you go from the first world to the second (but definitely not the third) with a jolt, as you drive the few yards that separate a country with a per capita GNP of around $35,000 from one of around $6,000.

What Julia saw was Spanish everywhere—on road signs, hoardings, storefronts, vans, the classroom language springing suddenly into three-dimensional life. "*Playa*—beach. *Camino*—road. *Abarrotes... Ceda el Paso... Cuota... Alto. Alto! Alto!*" *Alto* means "stop."

We took the fast seaside toll road that runs along the commercial strip from Tijuana south to Ensenada, past neo-Moorish *lotes*—condo blocks that offered American retirees a bargain taste of waterfront paradise beginning at $2,899 down and $320 a month, hotels with deterrent signs saying WELCOME SPRING-BREAKERS, dusty lots piled with fresh-from-the-kiln Aztec pottery (now I know where all those monster planters come from). The Baja peninsula, richer than mainland Mexico, floats high on the US tourist dollar. We stopped for lunch at a restaurant in La Mision, where Julia, blushing furiously, tried out her first phrases of beginner's Spanish and beamed with pride when she received a Spanish answer.

Beyond Ensenada, the road became a narrow, serpentine, two-lane blacktop where I had to slam on the brakes to let a tumbleweed twice our size roll past at a good 20 mph. We were waved through the military checkpoint that had northbound traffic backed up for a mile and more; a ritual exercise, meant to introduce some slowing friction to the stream of prohibited substances that pass this way into the United States. It's hard to imagine that the cartels are much impressed by the checkpoints, which mostly consist of soldiers bouncing vigorously on the trunks of cars and standing back to watch how the suspension goes up and down.

Our road—the road that had kept me awake at night for the last couple of weeks—was a turnoff a mile short of the village of Santo

Tomás, which followed the course of the Santo Tomás river down to the sea. I knew that it was nineteen miles long and I knew that it was rough. At the top, the most conspicuous building was a prosperous-looking tire repair shop. With just four inches clearance over the ground, the car wasn't designed for Mexican minor roads, and I took it at walking speed down this bumpy adventure of blind bends, potholes, ruts, rocks, gravel, and red dust.

The road kept to the contour dividing the arable from the barren: to the left, the irrigated river valley of chocolate-brown soil, with vineyards and vegetable plots; to the right, steep hills of shale, thinly furnished with sage, barrel cactus, agave, and yellow desert daisies. Pairs of roadrunners—the most uxorious birds I've ever seen, always going two by two—sprinted, quite unnecessarily, ahead of the car. Chicken vultures dawdled in the sky overhead. Break down on this road, I told my daughter, and the vultures pick you clean. At the end of an hour of intense, concentrated driving, watching for every rib and spur of rock, we had covered eight and a half miles.

Somewhere down near the sea an Easter party was coming to an end. Ruinous pickups, crammed full of teenagers in an elevated mood, bounced and swayed toward us at racetrack speeds, then slammed on their brakes to better enjoy the hilarious out-of-placeness of our car. Honking through the bends like Mr. Toad, I thought that if I were a soccer mom in an SUV I'd love this beautiful and eventful country drive, but my sentimental attachment to the exhaust system kept us to a wary crawl.

Barging shyly through families of plump cattle and horses with their foals, we reached the ocean at La Bocana, a cluster of wonky houses, mostly built of driftwood, and a litter-strewn sand berm across which the last few pie-eyed revelers were stumbling to their trucks. Three miles to go. The road, more or less level now, and graveled, snaked around the cliff edge to a bluff cove, terraced with plywood shacks that overlooked thirty or so open fishing boats, riding to their moorings among the rocks and kelp in a stiff offshore wind. Past the last shack was a scarred sign saying TERMINA CAMINO RURAL. I've been on lots of journeys, but none has finished with quite such satisfying decisiveness as this official End of the Road.

Though the end was also the beginning—of a pint-sized compound of sturdy tiled pink stucco bungalows set among palms and flowering cacti, a five-table cantina, and a triumphal mission-style arch, housing a church bell, and grandly titled Real Baja. "Resort" is the wrong word for Sam Saenz's charming, imaginative, and as yet rather unsuccessful attempt to divert the flow of Yanqui money from the highway and down the long rattletrap road to Puerto Santo Tomás. Stubborn dream would be a better term: Real Baja stands cheek-by-jowl with the fishermen's shacks of real Baja, holding out the promise of an alternative, service economy, powered by US dollars, not pesos. Sam Saenz believes in trickle-down, but to get the trickle you first need the flood, and so far nearly all that's come his way has been an intermittent dribble of American sportfishermen, drawn here by stories of trophy catches among the reefs.

He came out to greet us, ebulliently—as well he might, since Julia and I were his only guests, apart from a couple from Oakland who were camping nearby in a tent. Black-bearded, built like a skinny welterweight boxer, his skull wrapped in a red bandanna under a slouch hat, Saenz put us in his largest house, designed to sleep ten, which echoed with the busy noises of the sea beneath.

At the cantina, we were on our own: neither Francisco, who posed desultorily as our waiter, nor his wife, Maria, dark-skinned and tiny, who did the cooking, spoke a word of English. It was exactly as I'd hoped: Julia was pushed into the language at the deep end, sank for a few minutes, and came up swimming. With fish and lobsters from the bay, and wine and vegetables from the river valley, Maria's meals had the powerful flavor of place and terroir.

Sam Saenz joined us at the end of dinner. He was a Mexican-

American who'd returned to his ancestral roots after working in the California aerospace industry for thirty years. Born in Texas, one of fourteen children in a family of migrant farm laborers, he'd been drafted in the Korean War and gone to Michigan State University on the GI Bill. A passion for fishing and diving had led him to visit Puerto Santo Tomás in 1964. He's been involved with the place ever since. "I can't explain it. It hit me like a bomb. I just wanted to be here."

Laid off from the MX nuclear missile program in 1990, he moved to Baja to live full-time, and to put his engineering skills to use in the village, drilling wells, installing a solar-powered electrical system, hauling stones down from the hills to build cottages for visitors. Had it not been for those nineteen miles of lumpy, tire-gashing dirt road, he would have been very rich indeed by now.

"But we are remote."

Remote? With Americans gadding around their suburbs in high-riding four-wheel drive off-roaders, Puerto Santo Tomás hardly qualifies as being remote: if we could make it—comfortably, if slowly—in our car, it isn't remotely remote. But I shouldn't complain: nothing flatters the vanity of the tourist so much as arriving at an "unspoiled" place a few days ahead of the crowd.

Saenz explained the racial system that had vaguely troubled me over dinner. Little dark Maria was an indígena, Francisco a mestizo. The indígenos, from around Oaxaca and Yucatán, did much of the toilsome low-paid work in Baja, lured from their homes two thousand miles away by jobs in service, agriculture, and fishing.

"They are hard workers too. They give good value."

So the indígenos here were like Mexicans in the United States. For the next few days, I watched Francisco, always in a freshly pressed shirt, hang out with his friends around the pickup truck that served as their mobile club and bar, while his wife, her face an anxious knot, labored in the near dark of indoors, laundering, sweeping, cooking, and mothering their impish son, Luis. I saw Maria as the woman, broken by her cargo of flowers, in Diego Rivera's *The Lily Vendor*, and Francisco as the squarely planted male feet and crescent forehead visible behind her.

"The locals here, they've all worked in the US as illegals," Saenz said. "Like Francisco and Maria. But they don't want to learn English while they're there. They have no need: their boss is Mexican, they work on a Mexican team.... They live in Spanish. Then they come home."

"Like expats everywhere," I said. "Like Brits in Saudi Arabia, or Americans in Japan." It is a thorny subject, this, especially since the publication by Samuel (*Clash of Civilizations*) Huntington of his latest jeremiad, *The Hispanic Challenge*, which argues that Mexican immigration "threatens to divide the United States into two peoples" and represents a dangerous assault on "the Anglo-Protestant values that built the American dream." The Puerto Santo Tomás pattern of temporary exile and return may be more significant than Huntington and his like realize, and is a pattern unlikely to be reflected in the gross estimates of illegal immigration to the US.

After dinner, Saenz fired up the portable generator in his yard, got on his computer, and let Julia send an e-mail, via satellite dish, to her mother to say she'd arrived safely. With no television, no phone, no electricity or running water, Puerto Santo Tomás is on the Internet (which is how I found it), and Sam Saenz has his own Web site: www.puertosantotomas.com/.

The wind blew all night, fluting through the tiles of our house, and was blowing hard off the hills next morning, frosting the sea in the cove. The green-painted, high-bowed pangas shivered at the ends of their mooring lines—cockleshell craft, each about eight meters long with an outboard cocked on its stern.

"This is summer wind," Saenz said. "It never used to be like this. In the mornings, the bay should be flat calm in spring." The entire rainy season, from October to March, had brought just two inches of precipitation. In the river valley, the water table was dropping fast.

"It is a crisis for us. This summer, we will be in bad trouble."

Always the same story, of the wrong weather. From the shrinking snowpack of western Washington State through the unseasonable fog and heat of California to the drought of Baja, something was up with the climate and people were rattled. Lately, even the Bush administration has been making rattling noises, and in February 2004 a Pentagon report warned that imminent catastrophic climate change would lead to famine, floods, riots, and nuclear warfare: "Disruption and conflict will be endemic features of life.... Once again, warfare would define human life." Living with your own weather, it's tempting to chalk up the weird seasons to random climatic variation, but on a continuous drive like ours, through seventeen degrees of latitude of other people's weather, the ominous small symptoms of climate change are unignorable. It's said that the seeming gradualness of change in its early stages is fatally deceptive, that when the tipping point is reached disaster will unfold with the speed and force of a global avalanche.

Walking in the wind that shouldn't have been blowing, in the company of an eleven-year-old with the world before her, I thought of those long hot summers that famously precede major wars—all picnics and village cricket, before the unknowing villagers find themselves crouched miserably in some trench in Flanders, waiting for bullets with their names on them. Are we at that stage yet? It seems horribly probable.

Later, I took another walk with Rachel, one half of the Oakland couple in the tent, a plant ecologist who gave me some idea of the fragile complexity of what I had seen as undifferentiated chaparral brush. As she put names to the species around us—lovely names, such as pickleweed, coyote melon, Mormon tea, mallow, lamb's-quarters, desert hollyhock, creosote bush, and purple vetch—I imagined them frizzling to extinction on the hillside, leaving a last few spiny xerophytes to subsist on bare shale. Two inches of rain this year. How many—if any—next? The trouble with desert rainfall is that it leaves precious little margin for error, and it's likely to be land-scapes like this that will go first as the warming trend takes hold.

At least the fishermen were still in business. In winter, they dive for sea urchins, whose roes are prized in the Japanese sushi trade. In sum-mer, they fish offshore for albacore tuna, while the maze of inshore reefs provides a year-round supply of crustaceans, rock- and bottom-fish. NAFTA has been good for the fishermen, enabling them to export their catch from airports north of the border. Ross Perot's endlessly repeated line, in the 1992 presidential election, was that the effect of NAFTA would be "the giant sucking sound" of American jobs migrat-ing south to Mexico; a happier effect is the flappy, slithering sound of Mexican fish catching flights to Tokyo from San Diego International Airport.

The village of terraced shacks on the bluff was an all-male society, where the fishermen lived with khaki dogs who were kissing cousins to coyotes. Wives and children lived back in Ensenada (and in some cases much further away) where the women had jobs and the kids went to school, showing up in truckloads at Puerto Santo Tomás only on major holidays. So the men were hardly less separated from their families than the Mexican construction workers who labor on build-ing sites all over Seattle, sending money home each week to relatives they mostly see in creased photographs in their billfolds.

The fishermen tended their boats and tiny, dry gardens. One had painted a striking mural on the wall of his shack—a biblical scene of tall men in robes, out for a stroll in ancient Palestine, titled, in big black letters, *Hombres de valor*. The artist was a recently reformed character, now a passionate born-again Christian. His work was evidently intended to be a somewhat wishful-thinking picture of Puerto Santo Tomás and its diligent menfolk, sans their ever-ready bottles of Pacífico beer.

They had found for themselves an extraordinarily rich patch of sea. When another American family arrived in the village, we split the cost of hiring a fisherman named Lionel to take us out on his panga. I gave up fishing years ago, but Julia was avid to catch something. The trip cured her. The moment the anchor was down, off a reef a little way out from the shore, she was into a big one. Then another, and another, and another. With three rods out, the entire floor of the boat began to fill with writhing red rockfish, ocean whitefish, and calico bass. It was too easy, even for Julia, who, fearing that she wouldn't get a bite, found herself ankle-deep in whoppers. She palled of catching them, I got bored of photographing them, and it was a relief to step ashore and make a gift of the haul to Maria.

Next morning, as we loaded the car and faced the drive up the long dirt road to the highway, Sam Saenz was supervising the unloading of a truck laden with rocks. He was in the early stages of adding another pink house to his collection. About to turn seventy-one, he had an enviable belief in the future—as properly befitted a man whose youngest child (currently in Ensenada with her mother) was just eight weeks old. Tourists or no tourists, he was determined to build his Real Baja, with its neat Anglo-Spanish pun of "real" and "royal."

As we said goodbye to him, I realized suddenly why it had been our great good luck to light on Puerto Santo Tomás as our destination. For it was a distillation in miniature of the spirit of the West Coast. Sam Saenz, stubbornly building his little city by the sea, was kin to all the dreamers-into-being of unlikely western cities, from Junipero Serra to Bugsy Siegel, the megalomaniac creator of Las Vegas. Absence of water, absence of a natural harbor, absence of population have never deterred the Western Platonist with a vision. Pipe the water in! Crane the boats in and out of the sea! Only build, and the people will come! With such precedents, it's not really surprising that the architects of current US foreign policy believed they could transform Meso-potamia into an overnight free-market democracy—Vegas and LA on the shores of the Tigris and Euphrates, a triumph of the reckless, idealist American imagination. Throughout the length of our coastal drive we had passed through city after city raised in defiance of natural circumstances and conditions by someone of Saenz's ingenious and optimistic temperament.

And so it was with Puerto Santo Tomás's peculiar social fabric. Here was the migrant culture of the West, boiled down to its essence. Everyone, mestizo and indígeno alike, was from somewhere else, drawn here to make a killing from the sea or the river valley. The impermanent shacks of the village were exactly like the mining and logging camps that were the first western towns, and whose here-today-gone-tomorrow air still lingers in so many towns of the modern West. The asymmetrical society of men without women took one straight back to the West as it was in the nineteenth century.

As I suggested to Julia, western-born, in Puerto Santo Tomás she was looking at a mirror of her own regional past. The image in the mirror was tiny and stylized but essentially true. Look at this village in Baja now, and you can see Washington State and Oregon and California then—the camps, the men, the riches to be exploited, and someone in a broad-brimmed hat nursing a vision of how this improbable and obscure place is going to be the next big thing.

Two days later, I dropped Julia off in Los Angeles, where her mother was visiting and from where they'd fly back to Seattle, and drove home alone, across the northern end of the Mojave Desert, over the Sierras, through Nevada and California. Not far short of the Oregon border, I stopped for a beer at a tiny townlet in a wilderness of sage that had a post office, a tavern, and not much else. Its name was Likely.

Likely. No better name exists for the settlements of the far West than this word, pregnant with ironic shades and dubieties. "Having an appearance of truth or fact," says the OED: "apparently suitable," "promising," "handsome" (as in "likely lads"), "probable." Its own self-contradiction is built into the word, as in "Not likely!" or "A likely story." Likely would have been the right name for LA or Santa Barbara before they took off and the likely became proven, at least for now, at least so long as their supply of water holds out. Likely, California, despite its fine and friendly bar, has so far been largely disproven. Puerto Santo Tomás is a present Likely, its coming future still a gleam in one man's eye.

There's always been a strong element of the provisional about the West, and never more so than now, when likeliness is harder to calculate than ever before.

What Julia will see if, as promised, she takes this marvelous drive for herself in 2015 when she's twenty-two, is anybody's guess: cacti among the ruins would be my cheerless forecast, but I have a terrible record as a prophet and ardently hope that time will prove me wrong.

—May 2004

IO

RUNNING SCARED

DINNERTIME IS THE hour of the conspiracy theory here in Seattle. I've lost count of the times I've been told—always on excellent, but unnameable authority—that Osama bin Laden is already in American hands and that the Bush administration is waiting for the right moment to announce his capture. Ronald Reagan's body was on ice for many months, and his death was only announced when it became necessary to drive Abu Ghraib off the front page. Everybody knows, or thinks they know, that the administration will manipulate the intricate bells and whistles of homeland security to ensure the President's reelection. If terrorists don't strike in the run-up to November 2 (as most people assume they will) the level of alert will be jigged up to red, arrests will be made, the country will be declared saved from an evil plot and mass casualties, and Bush will storm past Kerry in the polls.

The latest theory comes hot from the mouths of anonymous agents in the Pakistan security service: the White House is putting immense pressure on the Musharraf regime to deliver "high-value targets," in the shape of bin Laden and Mullah Omar, on July 26, 27, or 28, to spectacularly eclipse the opening of the Democratic Party convention in Boston. Or, if that's too tall an order, they must be caught before polling day. My informant tells me that a senior Pakistani general, recently on a visit to D. C., said, "If we don't find these guys by the election, they're going to stick this whole nuclear mess up our asshole."

Much the most interesting thing about this last story is the character of my informant—not, as usual, Jack talking from the barbecue pit, but the sober *New Republic*, a magazine fiercely pro-Israel, which enthusiastically supported the invasion of Iraq. A respected senior editor, John B. Judis, is one of the three authors of the "July Surprise?" piece in the July 19 issue. Conspiracy theorizing is coming out of the Internet closet and going mainstream. Or, to put it another way, conspiracy theorizing is fast becoming a legitimate means of reporting on a government so secretive that unnamed Pakistani security types may well be the best-informed sources on the Bush administration's domestic policies and strategems.

Even before September 11, secrecy was this administration's hallmark, as when it invoked the principle of executive privilege to conceal from public view the proceedings of Vice President Cheney's energy task force. After September 11, secrecy was advanced, proudly, as a guiding principle for a nation at war. In his address to the joint session of Congress on September 20, 2001, Bush spoke of a new kind of war, "unlike any other we have ever known," that would include "covert operations, secret even in success." Donald Rumsfeld quoted Winston Churchill to the effect that in war "truth must be protected with a bodyguard of lies." Dick Cheney talked of a war to be fought "in the shadows: this is a mean, nasty, dangerous, dirty business. We have to operate in that arena." The great fear, shared by people not customarily given to paranoia, is that the Bush administration has taken these tactics for conducting a secret, asymmetric war and applied them wholesale to the day-to-day governance of the US.

To live in America now—at least to live in a port city like Seattle —is to be surrounded by the machinery and rhetoric of covert war, in which everyone must be treated as a potential enemy until they can prove themselves a friend. Surveillance and security devices are everywhere: the spreading epidemic of razor wire, the warnings in public libraries that the FBI can demand to know what books you're borrowing, the Humvee laden with troops in combat fatigues, the Coast Guard gunboats patrolling the bay, the pat-down searches and X-ray machines, the nondescript gray boxes equipped with radio antennae that are meant to sniff out pathogens in the air. It's difficult to leave the house now without encountering at least one of these reminders that we are being watched and that we live in deadly peril—though in peril of quite what is hard to say.

On May 26—a black day for sallow-skinned grocers and news vendors—the attorney general, John Ashcroft, flanked by FBI Director Robert S. Mueller, called a press conference to tell the nation of some "disturbing intelligence" that he'd recently received: preparations for an attack on the mainland US were 90 percent complete; likely targets included the upcoming G8 summit in Georgia, July 4 celebrations, and the Democratic and Republican conventions in Boston and New York. Al-Qaeda intended to "hit America hard." Mueller produced seven mugshots—six were of men of, as they say, Middle Eastern appearance—and told us to keep a sharp lookout for these "armed and dangerous" characters. For a few hours, the country shivered in anticipation of the horror about to descend on it, and phone lines to the FBI were jammed with excited descriptions of neighborhood news vendors and grocers.

Yet the color-coded alert system remained at yellow, and within the next couple of days it became clear that Ashcroft's disturbing new intelligence was many weeks old, and that much of it came from a discredited source—an Islamist propaganda site on the Internet well known to journalists for its daily stream of bloodcurdling boasts. Because Ashcroft had trespassed on the turf of Homeland Security chief Tom Ridge, and his freelance terror warning wasn't supported by the rest of the administration, we caught a rare glimpse of government Wizard of Ozzery at work. Ashcroft, it turned out, knew no more than the rest of us. Like us, he or his flunkies passed their time surfing the Net. When he told us that evidence for his grim warning had been "corroborated on a variety of levels," did he mean anything more than that it could be found on more than one Web site?

Ashcroft's performance confirmed the suspicion held by many that the Bush administration is in the cynical business of spreading generalized, promiscuous anxiety through the American populace, a sense of imminent but inexact catastrophe, for reasons that may have little to do with national security and much to do with political advantage. In the past three years, in the name of homeland security, a vast, coast-to-coast, combined surveillance and people-scaring apparatus has been assembled, on a scale, and with an intimate reach, never before seen in a democracy. The administration appears to be still learning to play this marvelous instrument, and wrong notes, such as those struck by Ashcroft, are common. But practice makes perfect.

Obsession with secrecy is a contagion directly transmitted from government to people. Just as the administration now moves in Cheney's arena of shadows, so masses of ordinary Americans are seeing themselves as self-appointed master spies, keeping watch on their government in the same covert way that the government supposedly keeps watch on al-Qaeda. The backyard barbecue sounds like a convention of spooks. "Chatter" has been heard, though its source can't be revealed... In such talk, Bush, Cheney & Co. are held to be as scheming, devious, and hard to catch as bin Laden himself.

The same tone is to be heard in current American journalism. On July 15, the solemnly judicious *New York Times* began a front-page story with the sentence, "In the annals of Washington conspiracy theories, the latest one, about vice-president Dick Cheney's future on the Republican ticket, is as ingenious as it is far-fetched." Buttering its bread lavishly on both sides, the paper went on to expend forty serious column inches on the far-fetched story. Since we can no longer get real news of the administration, we now get intelligence, which is something altogether different.

This accounts for liberal America's ready embrace of *Fahrenheit 9/11*, Michael Moore's slapdash confection of strong documentary footage and connect-the-dots paranoia. Whenever Moore puts himself in the center of the picture, he's pure Barbecue Man, brimming with "intel" that sounds even older and less reliable than that of Ashcroft. But Moore has rightly gauged the mood of his audience. People are hungry for classified information on their rulers, in part because their rulers are so busy collecting classified information on them, and *Fahrenheit 9/11* promotes the happy illusion that, for once, the magnetometers and security cameras have been turned on the President and his gang.

This is an extraordinary moment in American history. Half the country—including all the people I know best—believes it is trembling on the very lip of outright tyranny, while the other half believes that only the Bush administration stands between it and national collapse into atheism, socialism, black helicopters, and gay marriage. November 2 looms as a date of dreadful consequence. A bumper sticker, popular among the sort of people I hang out with, reads: BUSH-CHENEY '04—THE LAST VOTE YOU'LL EVER HAVE TO CAST. That's funny, but it belongs to the genre of humor in which the laugh is likely to die in your throat—and none of the people who sport the sticker on their cars are smiling. They are too busy airing conspiracy theories, which may or may not turn out to be theories.

—July 2004

I I

THE THREAT FROM THE SEA

"ROLL ON, THOU deep and dark blue ocean—roll!" wrote Byron in a comradely salute to the last great romantic wilderness on the planet. "...Man marks the earth with ruin—his control/Stops with the shore...." In 1818, he could hardly have foreseen that it would not be very long before man would mark the ocean, too, with ruin, poisoning whole seas with his industrial effluent, or fishing them out with vast synthetic nets deployed by immensely powerful hydraulic winches. Yet the sea is still wild: as global warming takes hold, shipwrecking storms are beginning to blow more fiercely, and with greater frequency, than they did in Byron's time, and the reach of the law of the land over the anarchy of the sea is, if anything, even more tenuous now than it was then. Mankind has always had much to fear from the ungovernable sea, and never more so than in this period of international terrorism, when who knows what abominations may soon arrive on our shores from the lawless terrain of the world's oceans.

The application of national law to events on the high seas was dealt with in a highly readable book by A. W. Brian Simpson, *Cannibalism and the Common Law*, published in 1984.[1] Simpson, now a professor

---

1. *Cannibalism and the Common Law: The Story of the Tragic Last Voyage of the* Mignonette *and the Strange Legal Proceedings to Which It Gave Rise* (University of Chicago Press, 1984).

of law at the University of Michigan, concentrated chiefly on the landmark case of *Regina* v. *Dudley and Stephens* (1884), which arose from the unhappy last voyage of the yacht *Mignonette*.

In mid-May 1884, the *Mignonette* sailed from Southampton, England, bound for Sydney, Australia, with a crew of four professional seamen who were commissioned to deliver the boat to her new Australian owner. On July 5 she was wallowing in a violent storm in the South Atlantic when a poorly timed maneuver put her broadside-on to a huge breaking sea. The force of the wave broke away the bulwarks and a section of planking on the leeward side; as the yacht quickly sank, the crew scrambled into a cockleshell dinghy, taking with them basic navigational instruments and two cans of turnips as their only provisions. They had heaved a half-full water cask into the sea, hoping to pick it up later, but it disappeared from sight.

On July 9, they caught a passing turtle and ate it, bones and all. By July 21 there was talk of drawing lots to decide which of themselves should be killed for food, though it seems that no draw probably took place. On July 24, the captain, Tom Dudley, a devout Anglican churchgoer, took his penknife to the throat of the seventeen-year-old cabin boy, Richard Parker, severing the jugular vein and catching his blood in the ship's chronometer case. On July 29, while the survivors were still dining on the remains of young Parker, they were spotted by a passing German ship, and taken back to England, where the captain and mate (the deckhand escaped prosecution because he was needed as a witness for the Crown) were put on trial for murder.

Legally speaking, a ship is much like a floating embassy, a detached chunk of the land whose flag it flies, so that seamen aboard a British ship are subject to the same laws that govern their brethren ashore. *The Mignonette* was a registered British ship, and had the act of cannibalism taken place aboard the yacht, there would have been no question about whether an English court had jurisdiction in the matter. But, as the defense counsel for the crew argued, Richard Parker had been killed in the dinghy, not a registered ship, in international waters, so that no court, English or otherwise, could rightly try a case concerning an act committed in a wilderness without laws. This ingenious proposition was not well stated by the defense counsel, Arthur—soon to be Sir Arthur—Collins, QC, who bungled most of his best arguments in the trial. The judges made no sense of it at all, but in his book Brian Simpson gives that first line of defense more weight than it was credited with at the time.

The second line of defense (again far better put by Simpson than by counsel) was that the situation in which the men found themselves at sea was so extreme that the law of the land could hardly apply to it:

> In desperate conditions, such as those confronting Dudley and Stephens [the mate aboard the *Mignonette*], men are reduced by circumstances to a state in which it is incongruous to think of laws applying at all. They are in a state of nature, where there are no legal rights, duties, or crimes.... Laws exist to regulate social arrangements in normal conditions, not in wholly abnormal conditions when society breaks down. Arthur Collins toyed with this approach, but he never formulated the idea at all clearly. The judges seem to have been quite incapable of grasping it....

The befuddled judges in the courtroom were anxiously trying to counter popular opinion expressed in the dockside pubs of England, where there was little doubt that the trial was an outrage. The lore, as opposed to the law, of the sea was quite clear: so long as lots had been properly drawn beforehand, the crew of the *Mignonette* had obeyed the rules and could not be guilty of a crime. Public sympathy was with the men and against the lawyers. The sea had its own code of justice, and the lubberly invasion of men in wigs and gowns was resented as an impertinent trespass on hallowed maritime tradition, in which "survival cannibalism" was an accepted social practice.

The newspapers of the time sided with the judges: the idea that the sea was a realm beyond law, at a time when the sea afforded the arterial highway system of the British Empire, was a dangerous affront to the order of things. As *The Spectator* editorialized:

> The conviction that such murders are justified by the law of self-defence, and are not, therefore, illegal, is so general amongst seafaring men, and has so infected naval literature, that a solemn judgement to the contrary, pronounced by more than one judge, has become indispensable.

The jury found the men guilty of murder as charged, but pleaded for mercy on their behalf. The judge then sentenced them to death—though he did not put on the traditional black cap while doing so. The sentence was almost immediately commuted to one of six months' imprisonment without hard labor. So society was protected from the wild customs of the sea by the most solemn pronouncement in the English lawbook ("You [will] be taken to the prison where you came, and that on a day appointed for the purpose of your execution you be there hanged by the neck until you be dead"), while the sea-lawyers in the pubs were mollified by the shortness of the jail time actually served for the offense. Captain Tom Dudley earned the ultimate accolade of Victorian celebrity: Madame Tussaud's found space for his wax effigy.

Simpson's book, which ranges far and wide in its discussion of gory tales of men in dire straits at sea, memorably documents the fraying of law as it reaches out into international waters. The cherished principle of "the freedom of the high seas" is barely separable from the troubling fact that the ocean is a licentious wilderness where people have always been able to get away with doing things they could not do on land.

* * *

Fresh from reporting on chaos at the site of the twin towers in *American Ground*,[2] William Langewiesche has taken on the rampant legal chaos of the sea in the twenty-first century. *The Outlaw Sea*[3] is in part a sequence of lucid and often thrilling stories about recent founderings, groundings, and acts of piracy. It is also an unsettling appraisal of the laws, treaties, conventions, traditions, and organizations which, meant to regulate the sea, succeed largely in creating myriad loopholes for ingenious rogues to exploit. According to Langewiesche, the watery seven tenths of the globe are littered with some 143,000 ships: most sail under "flags of convenience," registered in such countries as the island state of Tuvalu in the Pacific; many are dangerous rust buckets, nearly all are undermanned, with crews on third-world wages. The owners of these vessels, hidden behind multiple fronts and shell companies, are hard—and sometimes impossible —to trace. Though there now exists an International Law of the Sea (still not ratified by the US) and its enforcing body, the International Maritime Organization, the best efforts to police the sea have so far proved alarmingly ineffective. Meanwhile, as Langewiesche dryly notes, Osama bin Laden and his associates "are in the shipping business," with a considerable fleet of elderly freighters. The whereabouts and identities of these much-sought-after ships are unknown: in the way of the sea, their present names, and the flags they now sail under, are buried so deep in an ocean of misleading paperwork that they are beyond discovery.

The flag of convenience—that flimsiest of legal fictions—bears much of the blame for the lawless state of the sea. Few ships engaged in international trade have ever come within sight of the port of registration displayed on their sterns. Vessels owned and operated by entities within the US and the European Union go about the world as

---

2. *American Ground: Unbuilding the World Trade Center* (Diane, 2002).

3. *The Outlaw Sea: A World of Freedom, Chaos, and Crime* (North Point, 2004).

detached chunks of Liberia or Belize, subject to the tolerant provisions of Liberian or Belizian law on manning, pay, maintenance, and safety. Owners of fishing boats have lately taken to reflagging in order to evade onerous conservation measures enacted by their actual home countries. It is a marvelous, Alice-in-Wonderland-like system, and irresistible to prudently cost-conscious shipowners and scheming lawbreakers alike.

Langewiesche says that the practice

> began in the early days of World War II as an American invention sanctioned by the United States government to circumvent its own neutrality laws. The idea was to allow American-owned ships to be re-flagged as Panamanian and used to deliver materials to Britain without concern that their action (or loss) would drag the United States unintentionally into war.

My understanding is that reflagging for base commercial reasons began well before World War II, and seamen's unions in the US fought against it in the 1930s. Interestingly, Joseph Conrad's *Typhoon* (1902) begins with the ominous reflagging of the steamship *Nan-Shan*, whose colonial British owners, Messrs. Sigg and Son, "judged it expedient to transfer her to the Siamese flag." Mr. Jukes, the first mate, is affronted by the new flag, which tellingly sports a white elephant on a red ground, though the dim and literal-minded Captain MacWhirr—Conrad's model of the new breed of machine-age captains—sees nothing wrong with it. Determined to keep to schedule and save Messrs. Sigg the cost of the extra coal required to steam around the edge of the storm, MacWhirr insists on driving his ship straight through the center of the typhoon. It's part of Conrad's purpose that we associate the multiple misfortunes that befall the *Nan-Shan*, and her miserable cargo of two hundred Chinese coolies, with the "queer flag" under which she sails, beyond the reach and protection of English law. At the end of the story, Jukes writes a letter to a friend, complaining that the reflagging had left the ship in a situation of precarious legal solitude:

> It is an infernally lonely state for a ship to be going about the China seas with no proper consul, not even a gunboat of her own anywhere, nor a body to go to in case of some trouble.

As Conrad clearly saw more than a hundred years ago, reflagging turns ships into lawless orphans—unruly ragamuffins of the sea.

At least there was (in the wishful phrase of the International Law of the Sea) a genuine link between the *Nan-Shan* and her flag state of Siam. No such link usually exists now. Langewiesche nicely outlines the blithe comedy of convenience flagging:

> Panama is the largest maritime nation on earth, followed by bloody Liberia, which hardly exists. No coastline is required either. There are ships that hail from La Paz, in landlocked Bolivia. There are ships that hail from the Mongolian desert. Moreover, the registries themselves are rarely based in the countries whose names they carry: Panama is considered to be an old-fashioned "flag" because its consulates handle the paperwork and collect the registration fees, but "Liberia" is run by a company in Virginia, "Cambodia" by another in South Korea, and the proud and independent "Bahamas" by a group in the City of London.

During the course of its career, a ship is likely to run through a string of names and flag states, changing its identity at the owner's whim, quite conceivably during the course of a single voyage, so that the freighter *Jane* might leave Baltimore harbor registered in Tuvalu and arrive in Marseilles as the *Emma* of the Cayman Islands. One story that regularly makes the rounds of the docks is of the ship (locally owned, and you're supposed to have heard of it) that sailed away a few months ago and was reported lost at sea; in fact, as the storyteller happens to know, it was in a mid-ocean calm when the crew brought out the paint pots and the new flag. The insurance money added up to many millions. The ship is sailing under a new alias and nationality. True or not, the story isn't half as implausible as it ought to be.

If the identity of a ship is potentially fluid in the extreme, the identity of its owner is hardly less so. Langewiesche cites the case of the *Erika*, an aging tanker, registered in Malta, that broke in two off the Brittany coast while it was transporting 22,000 tons of oil from Dunkirk to Livorno in Italy, coating miles of French beaches in black sludge. The captain claimed "that he himself had no idea who the owners were"; his only dealings had been with a management company in Ravenna, Panship Management & Services:

> Panship worked for the ship's registered owner, Tevere Shipping of Valletta, Malta, which in turn was held by two other companies, Agosta Investments and Financiers Shipping, both of 80 Broad Street, Monrovia, Liberia. Somehow in the constellation of names behind this single ship there appeared to be still other companies—in Switzerland, the Bahamas, Panama, and England. There were various banks too, including one in Scotland and a Swiss branch of France's Credit Agricole. After a month of trying to follow these connections, the official French inquiry admitted defeat.

Eventually the shipping newspaper *Lloyd's List* traced ownership of the *Erika* to a cheerful Italian named Giuseppe Savarese who professed to be "bemused" by the hue and cry, and boasted of the excellent condition of the ship at the time she broke up at sea. (A month later, in January 2000, Savarese was in trouble again with another badly corroded vessel, the Maltese-registered *Maria S.*, which was detained in Sicily. By August 2000, when she was impounded in Amsterdam, the *Maria S.* had become the Mauritian-owned, Bolivian-registered *Sandrien.*)

Trying to impose order on this world is like tidying spilled mercury. As Langewiesche amply illustrates, mandatory inspections of seaworthiness are commonly passed with honors by ships that should properly be classified as hazardous waste. After September 11 the Bush administration made the US Coast Guard a branch of the Department of Homeland Security, and since then American efforts to regulate shipping bound for US ports have taken on an air of panicked urgency. So far, though, these efforts have produced little more than piles of new forms for captains to fill in, along with airy assurances that all will soon be well:

> There is unembarrassed talk in Washington of a future under control, in which sailors will undergo meaningful background checks and will be supplied with unforgeable, biometrically verifiable IDs by honest, appropriately equipped, and cooperative governments. Panama, for instance, will vouch for the integrity of, say, an Indonesian deckhand working on a ship operated by a Cayman Island company on behalf of an anonymous Greek. This is a vision so disconnected from reality that it might raise questions about the sanity of the United States.

In Rotterdam, Langewiesche spoke to a Dutch maritime official who had watched the recently introduced American system of preinspection of containers before they are craned aboard:

> "Look, if you want to send a bomb through, it's so simple! The chances of it being filtered out are almost nil!" He was not being critical so much as flatly descriptive. As a believer in good government, but long exposed to the chaos of the ocean, he seemed

to have learned the hard lesson that government tools might simply not apply.

Most readers of Langewiesche's book will come away with vivid memories of particular disasters at sea: the breaking up of the Maltese-registered *Kristal* off the Atlantic coast of Spain in 2001; the boarding by pirates of the Japanese-registered *Alondra Rainbow* in the Malacca Straits in 1999, and the subsequent reappearance of that ship as the Belize-flagged *Mega Rama* off the coast of India a few weeks later; and, most spectacularly, the foundering of the huge car ferry *Estonia* in the Baltic in 1994 with a loss of at least 852 lives. A shipwreck—or an act of piracy—is a complex sequence of events, requiring the author who describes it to be everywhere at once, as well as to be in confident possession of arcane technical knowledge about ship design and construction, navigation and shiphandling, and the effects of wind on water in heavy weather. In addition, the author needs to have a novelist's ability to sketch the responses of individual characters to situations of extreme stress.

The literature of the sea is filled with examples of writers who have failed to measure up to these exacting demands, and it's a pleasure to report that Langewiesche's book satisfies on every count. He has the enviable ability to distill from an intimidating mass of information, derived from official inquiries and interviews with survivors, narratives of extraordinary clarity without a trace of jargon, and laced with detached wit. He appears to be equally at home in the wheelhouse of a violently pitching ship and in the mazy outer reaches of maritime law.

His account of the sinking of the *Estonia*, and of the international inquiry that followed, is a magnificently succinct piece of bravura reporting. One might compare it to Walter Lord's excellent book on the *Titanic*, *A Night to Remember* (1955), but Langewiesche is a more accomplished prose stylist than Lord, and his grasp of technical detail is surer. He is also a cunning literary architect: even as we're engrossed in the page-turning drama of the loss of a great ship in a storm, we are never allowed to lose sight of the fact that the drama is just one more strand of a larger argument about the failure of the land to comprehend, let alone control, the chaotic nature of the sea.

The *Estonia* (formerly the *Viking Sally*, *Silja Star*, and *Wasa King*), built in Germany, registered both in Tallinn, the Estonian capital, and in Cyprus, and owned jointly by a company fronting for the Estonian state and a Swedish shipping line, went down off the archipelagic coast of southwest Finland while en route from Tallinn to Stockholm. The governments of Sweden, Finland, and Estonia immediately set up a Joint Accident Investigation Commission to establish the cause of the disaster; not, at first sight, a very difficult task, since it soon became clear that the hinged bow visor—the portion of the bow that swings upward to allow vehicles to drive on or off—had sheared off, allowing the sea unhindered access to the car decks. In the event, the commission, with its panels of experts from all three nations, sat for three long and inconclusive years, listening to lawyers telling rival stories.

Among the causes advanced were that the bow visor had been badly designed by the German shipbuilder; that it had been poorly maintained by the Estonians, who had allowed its rubber seal to rot, and thereby destroyed the integrity of the bow structure; that the Soviet-trained Estonian captain could not tell port from starboard, and had driven his ship with reckless disregard for sea and weather and with callous lack of concern for his passengers; that negligent safety inspectors (Estonians again) were to blame; that a bomb had blown the bow visor out of the ship, and that another had put a hole below the waterline on her starboard side. A German journalist and filmmaker, Jutta Rabe, had the most elaborate explanation. In Langewiesche's words:

Rogue elements in Russia had sold a secret weapon to the Pentagon and were getting it to the United States by smuggling it to Stockholm in a truck on the ferry. A Russian scientist with a briefcase full of sensitive documents was along for the ride. To keep the deal from going through, former KGB agents boarded the ship, and shot the scientist, the captain, and a sailor on the car deck. Then they placed charges against the bow door locks and the hull, detonated them, and escaped in a lifeboat. Afterward, the Swedes, Finns, and Estonians caved in to an American-led cover-up so intense that it included the need to "disappear" the ship's relief captain, who had survived but somehow knew too much.

Ms. Rabe, who has made a string of short documentaries and a full-length feature film (*Baltic Storm*) about the *Estonia*, was matched in her obsessive zealotry by Peter Holtappels, the lawyer representing the shipbuilders, whose splendidly detailed account of the sinking exonerated his clients from the least scintilla of blame. The Holtappels story also allowed for the possibility of a bomb.

So the *Estonia* sank for the second time, in a sea of paper. The Joint Accident Investigation Commission found out many things but was unable to reconcile them into a coherent explanation of why the tragedy had happened. It made its recommendations, few of which would ever be acted upon. What mainly emerged from its proceedings was, as usual, the shady and irregular character of the sea and everything that happens there.

Langewiesche repeatedly touches on but does not discuss in any great detail the issue of maritime terrorism. Plausible fears of a seaborne dirty bomb, dispersing a toxic cloud of ricin or cesium-137 across a city, are rapidly changing the culture of American ports. Seattle, where I live, is a prime example.

Before September 11, Seattle, squatting possessively on its long and placid fjord, looked to the sea for good news: for immense hauls of Pacific salmon, for Klondike miners (fools easily parted from their money), for all the benefits of trade with Asia. The city lay innocently open to the sea, seeing in every next container ship, as it rounded West Point and made the turn into Elliott Bay, the prospect of more money in Seattle's coffers.

That is no longer so. The container terminal on Harbor Island, once the place where parents took their children for their first driving lessons on its wide and empty spaces, has become a fortress of new concrete walls, new razor wire, new chain-link fencing. Armed Coast Guard vessels patrol Elliott Bay. Each arriving ship is scrutinized as a potential bearer of very bad news.

Seattle is a target—at least the Department of Homeland Security believes it to be so. In the first round of federal grants to "high risk, high density urban areas," Seattle was one of seven cities singled out for largesse (the others were New York, Chicago, Washington, D. C., Houston, Los Angeles, and San Francisco). Last May, Homeland Security, the Justice Department, the FBI, and several other agencies mounted a dress rehearsal for terrorist catastrophe code-named TOPOFF 2 and designed to test the preparedness of the emergency services. Chicago and Seattle were selected for the exercise. In Chicago, the attack came from the air, with a crop sprayer dropping the germs of pneumonic plague over the city; in Seattle it came from the sea, as a dirty bomb hidden in a container blew up on Harbor Island. Several city blocks were cordoned off and littered with broken glass, overturned buses, and smoking wreckage to simulate the effects of the blast. The victims were played by actors and volunteers: the "dead" were carted off on gurneys to the morgue, while "survivors" were taken to Harborview Hospital to be decontaminated. The two-city exercise (in which much went wrong) was monitored via satellite in Washington, D. C.

Seattle offers a great temptation to terrorists. Its container terminal is more snugly integrated with its downtown than in any other port in the United States. A good pitcher, standing on the docks, could hit Safeco Stadium, where the Seattle Mariners have taken to losing on a grand scale this year. The banking and insurance towers of the business district are comfortably within a one-mile radius of the port. It's no wonder that the city has lately broken out in a rash of anxious surveillance devices, from CCTV cameras to the nondescript gray boxes with funnels that measure pathogens in the air.

More than most places, Seattle has reason to be aware of the lawlessness of the sea. In the course of sixteen days around the turn of the millennium, the Immigration and Naturalization Service, acting on tip-offs, raided four ships arriving at Harbor Island from Hong Kong, and found a total of sixty illegal Chinese immigrants hidden in containers. It wasn't clear who had alerted the INS and why (perhaps a gang war on the Chinese mainland had led to anonymous phone calls to the American authorities), but for just a few weeks a window was opened on a major smuggling route. The would-be immigrants were paying (or owing) around $40,000 for the trip, and the intercepted containers must have represented only a tiny fraction of what was evidently a huge and generally successful trade. As the deputy director of the INS told *The Seattle Times* in January 2000:

> Containers are deceptively difficult. They are a problem.... Containers bring a flow of legitimate business, and criminals do learn to take advantage of them.

Even now, it is said that only 2 percent of containers have their contents inspected before they are shipped, and that is probably an optimistic estimate. A more thorough and time-consuming system of inspection would threaten to bring international trade to a standstill, and would in any case be unlikely to deter a terrorist bent on shipping, say, two flat sheets of the plastic explosive Semtex with a radiological or biological payload. A single ship can carry up to 4,000 containers, while the average container has a capacity of 2,720 cubic feet—a vast space in which to secrete an object as compact as a dirty bomb would probably be. The port cities of the United States have good reason to feel uneasy.

On July 1, the federal government's long-trumpeted Operation Safe Commerce came into force, and of the 265 ships arriving from abroad in US ports that day, six foreign-flagged vessels were denied entry by the Coast Guard because their paperwork was not in order. Tom Ridge has described the new measures as "creating a culture of security in ports around the world," but their real impact is more frankly characterized by William Langewiesche:

> The only sure effect of the new regulations is that legitimate operators, who do not pose a threat, will comply. But it is likely that terrorists will comply as well, and that, like many shipowners today, they will evade detection not by ducking procedures and regulations, but by using them to hide. This would be very easy to do. Paradoxically, when a ship approaching US shores does not comply, it will be because it is a bumbler, and therefore almost by definition innocent.

Asymmetric or "fourth-generation" warfare pits a nation-state against an enemy who is everywhere and nowhere; who has no flag, no uniformed army, no capital city, no ascertainable geography. For such an enemy, the sea is the friendliest place on earth, the natural habitat of the stateless terrorist. Its legal ambiguities suit him perfectly; it offers secrecy, anonymity, and the ability to change identity at will; it is one enormous hiding place. The lax internationalism of the ocean might have been expressly designed to accommodate the kind of loose, far-flung, fugitive, paranational organization that may now confront us. The rusty cargo ship is a potential weapon that could deliver death on a considerably greater scale than September 11 —and the chances of a ship reaching the heart of its chosen target city without being detected are so high that they hardly bear thinking about.

As Langewiesche makes frighteningly clear, there is very little that governments can do to regulate nefarious activities on the high seas. (Coastal waters are of course another matter.) The tempting first step would be a concerted international effort to end the practice of reflagging—something that might take, at best, a generation to achieve, and could well prove in the end to have been hardly worth doing, since all it would accomplish in practice would be to establish genuine "links" between ships and their flag states (and rogue states have flags too). The lesson of Langewiesche's book is that the most rigid law turns soggy and pliable as soon as it extends beyond the twelve-mile territorial limit. And no law of the sea, ratified by however many nations, could keep al-Qaeda or its kindred spirits out of the shipping business.

—August 2004

12

PASTOR BUSH

IN THE SECULAR, liberal, top-left-hand corner of the US where I live, the prevailing mood was one not far short of despair as incredulity mounted that the daily avalanche of bad news from Baghdad, Fallujah, Tikrit, Samarra, Najaf, Nasiriyah, Kufa, Ramadi, Baquba, and elsewhere was apparently failing to make any significant dent in Bush's poll numbers, or expose his claim that freedom and democracy are on the march in Iraq as a blithe and cynical fiction. What would it take? people asked. How many more American and Iraqi deaths? When would it sink in that the occupation of Iraq is a bloody catastrophe? Why was the electorate so unmoved by the abundant empirical evidence that the administration's policy in the Middle East wantonly endangers America as it endangers the wider world? Kerry's performance in the first presidential debate brought a much-needed lift of spirits to this neck of the woods, but the Democratic candidate is up against something more formidable than the person of George Bush: he has to deal with the unquiet spirit of American Puritanism and its long and complicated legacy.

Last Monday, on the school run, I caught an interview on NPR's *Morning Edition* with the grieving family of a sergeant in the Oregon National Guard who was killed in Iraq on September 13. Here's what Sergeant Ben Isenberg's dad said:

This war is not about Iraqis and Americans, or oil: this is a spiritual war. The people who don't understand that just need to dig into their Bible and read about it. It's predicted, it's predestined. Benjamin understood that the President is a very devouted [*sic*] Christian. Ben understood that the calling was to go because the President had the knowledge, and understood what was going on, and it's far deeper than we as people can ever really know. We don't get the information that the President gets.

In context it's clear that by "information" he wasn't talking about the stuff that passes from the CIA to the White House. This information comes from the guy whom Bush likes to call his "higher Father." As the President said in the closing lines of his acceptance speech at the Republican convention last month, "We have a calling from beyond the stars..."—a claim that in some societies might lead to a visit from the men in white coats, but in America, among the faithful, is met with rapturous applause.

Every Bush speech is richly encrypted with covert biblical allusions and other secret handshakes with his fundamentalist listeners, but one need not be a fundamentalist to warm to this sort of religiose rhetoric, for it is every bit as much of an "American" thing as it is a "Christian" one. Rationalist liberals, tone-deaf to its appeal, make a serious mistake in their assumption that facts on the ground, in Iraq or in the domestic US, can readily explode what the Bush administration has managed to project as a matter not of reason but of faith.

Faith, as Mark Twain's apocryphal schoolboy said, "is believing what you know ain't so." Faith always contradicts the visible evidence, like the putrefying body or the fossil in the rock—obstacles put in our way to test the mettle of our belief and reveal the inadequacy of our merely sublunar knowledge. Ben Isenberg's father was certain of this: "It's far deeper than we as people can ever really know."

No culture in the world has elevated "faith," in and of itself, with or without specific religious beliefs, to the status it enjoys in the United States. Faith—in God, or the future, or the seemingly impossible, which is the core of the American dream—is a moral good in its own right. In no other culture is the word "dream" so cemented into everyday political language, for in America dreams are not idle, they are items of faith, visions that transcend the depressing available evidence and portend the glorious future as if it were indeed "predicted... predestined," as Isenberg's father saw the war on Iraq.

When Americans tell their own history at the grade-school, storybook level, they conveniently forget the earliest and most successful colony of tobacco aristocrats in Virginia (a bunch of degenerate smokers) and instead trace themselves back to the zealous theocrats in tall black hats who founded the Massachusetts Bay Colony, and whose first harvest is celebrated in the all-American orgy of Thanksgiving. The names of the *Susan Constant*, *Godspeed*, and *Discovery*, which put into the James River in 1607, have little resonance now, but everyone knows about the 1620 voyage of the *Mayflower* and its Pilgrim Fathers because the Puritans, who have never gone out of date, left behind a peculiarly American philosophy of the miraculous power of faith and hard labor, along with a dangerously uplifting vision of America's rightful place in the world. In a sermon of 1651, Peter Bulkeley laid out the essential rhetorical frame of Bush's foreign policy:

> We are as a city set upon a hill, in the open view of all the earth, the eyes of the world are upon us because we profess ourselves to be a people in covenant with God.... Let us study so to walk that this may be our excellency and dignity among the nations of the world among which we live; that they may be constrained to say of us, only this people is wise, a holy and blessed people.... We are the seed that the Lord hath blessed.

The sting in that exclusive "only" has been lately felt by almost every foreign ambassador to the UN who's had to listen to Bush or Powell lecturing the assembly on America's historic moral exceptionalism.

It was axiomatic to Puritan belief that the city on the hill had been raised in a land previously inhabited by devils whose spirits still walked abroad, conspiring against the holy, wise, and blessed citizens. At the time of the Salem witch trials in 1693, Cotton Mather struck exactly the same note as Bush strikes when he speaks of al-Qaeda:

> The devil is now making one attempt more upon us; an attempt more difficult, more surprising, more snarled with unintelligible circumstances than any we have hitherto encountered; an attempt so critical, that if we get well through, we shall soon enjoy halcyon days, with all the vultures of hell trodden under our feet.

A "horrible plot" had been detected, "which if it were not seasonably uncovered would probably blow up and pull down all the churches in the country." More than twenty-one witches "have confessed that they have signed unto a book, which the devil showed them, and engaged in his hellish design of bewitching and ruining our land."

While the Virginia colony brought eighteenth-century rationalism to America, and supplied four of its first five presidents (Washington, Jefferson, Madison, and Monroe), the New England Puritans of Massachusetts gave Americans an intensely dramatic and emotional sense of their peculiar predicament. They were an exception among nations, uniquely favored by Providence. They alone enjoyed the liberty to walk with God according to their own lights. They were a people of faith beleaguered on all sides by wicked spirits. Cleaving to their faith, they must distrust "imperfect reason" (Mather's phrase) as a means of discerning the mystery of creation and the visible world around them. Not least, the Puritan plain style (Mather warned writers of "muses no better than harlots" and of prose "stuck with as many jewels as the gown of a Russian ambassador"), which owed much to the teaching of Peter Ramus, the French philosopher and rhetorician, made these ideas accessible to the least educated, and gave them the unvarnished vigor that they still have today. The remarkable survival of this seventeenth-century worldview in twenty-first-century America has as much to do with style as with theological substance: people who would now find Jefferson or Madison hard going could easily thrill to the words of Mather, John Winthrop, the rollicking hellfire poet Michael Wigglesworth, or the poet of domestic sublimity Anne Bradstreet.

The Puritans live. And the shrewd men and women of the Bush administration have expertly hot-wired the President to the galvanic energy source of Puritan tradition. It's as if America, since September 11, has been reconstituted as a colonial New England village: walled in behind a stockade to keep out Indians (who were seen as in thrall to the devil); centered on its meeting house in whose elevated pulpit stands Bush, the plain-spun preacher, a figure of nearly totalitarian authority in the community of saints. The brave young men of the village are out in the wilderness, doing the Lord's work, fighting wicked spirits who would otherwise be inside the stockade, burning down Main Street and the meeting house. That, at least, is how the presidential handlers have tried to paint things, and, given the continuing power of the American Puritan tradition, it's not very surprising that a likely electoral majority have gratefully accepted the picture at its face value: that the proportions are all wrong (the world's remaining superpower simply won't fit into the space of a pious, beleaguered village) doesn't matter, for the administration has successfully tapped into a toxic national mythos.

Faith rules. After a faltering start to his presidency, Bush found his role in the aftermath of the attacks of September 2001 as America's pastor in chief. His inarticulacy without a script was an earnest of his humility and sincerity, his dogmatic certitude a measure of his godly inspiration. "His way of preaching was very plain," as Mather wrote of John Eliot of Roxbury, Massachusetts. "He did not starve [the people] with empty and windy Speculations." Confronted a couple of weeks ago with the CIA's grim forecast of mounting unrest and possible civil war in Iraq, Bush airily said, "They were just guessing." The President doesn't guess. As he intimates to his congregation on every possible occasion, his intelligence is leaked to him by He Who Holds the Stars in His Right Hand.

To doubt is to succumb to temptation by the wicked spirits. In the New Testament, empiricism gets a bad press in the person of poor Thomas Didymus, and Christ's rebuke: "Blessed are they that have not seen, and yet have believed." That the facts on the ground in Iraq are in clear contradiction of all Bush's claims about the flowering of liberty and democracy there is merely one of those tests of faith to which all true believers are subject. Of course we can't see it, but that makes the miracle only more marvelous, its very invisibility an inspiring moral challenge for the faithful.

In last Thursday's debate with Kerry at the University of Miami, Bush appeared petulant and bemused (especially in the reaction shots that were shown by the networks in defiance of the rules agreed on by the Commission on Presidential Debates) to find himself there at all. There's no space in the meeting house for two rival pulpits, and Pastor Bush, for the first time since his election, if that's the right term for what happened in 2000, had to endure standing on an equal footing with an upstart congregant who was the spitting image of Doubting Thomas. There was a note of wounded incredulity in Bush's voice when he said of Kerry that "he changes positions on something as fundamental as what you believe in your core, in your heart of hearts, is right in Iraq." O faithless Kerry!—apostate!—unbeliever! In Bush's Puritan theology, to change one's mind in the face of overwhelming evidence is tantamount to denying the very God who rules your "heart of hearts." How can my belief be wrong if He placed it there?

Yet debates—even ones as stilted as those agreed on between the campaigns this year—are rational exercises with an inbuilt bias favoring reason over faith. Unsurprisingly, the rationalist on Thursday beat the preacher at the rationalist's own game, and in my own political neighborhood there was hardly less elation that evening than if the Seattle Mariners had carried off the World Series. But a debate is a very different thing from an election, and if Kerry did manage to win on November 2, it would be a surprising triumph of cold reason over hot religious mythology.

No more classic American sentiment has ever been put into a foreigner's mouth than when the New York lyricist Joe Darion made Don Quixote sing, in *Man of La Mancha*, "To dream the impossible dream,/To fight the unbeatable foe,/To bear with unbearable sorrow,/To run where the brave dare not go." Only an entrenched belief in one's own exceptionalism and a wonder-working Providence could justify such otherwise self-evidently futile activities. With Bush, we're now dreaming an impossible dream and fighting an unbeatable foe, and tens of millions of Americans—enough, quite probably, to give Bush a second term—believe that is the right, because it's the American, thing to do.

Tony Blair has lately given the impression that he's been channeling the same source (Almighty God and/or Karl Rove) that inspires the rhetoric of Bush, but in Britain there is no rich mulch of popular national tradition in which Blair's words can take root. The historic connection between the Labour Party of Keir Hardie's time and the Methodist Church is something altogether different from the great folk memory of the embattled God-fearing city on the hill that stirs deep in the American imagination. When Bush plays the faith card, he summons powerful ancient ghosts. When Blair tries to bring off the same trick, he merely calls attention to his conscience, his private religious beliefs, awakening no echoes in the land of mild, secularized Anglicanism where to speak of one's own intimacy with God's purpose is to place oneself in the embarrassing company of the man in the ragged overcoat, haranguing a nonexistent audience from a soapbox at Speakers Corner—which, come to think of it, is a convenient short stroll from the Blair family's new quarters in Connaught Square.

—October 2004

13

AMERICA'S REALITY CHECK

HERE IN SEATTLE, most people I know are sick with anxiety about the outcome of Tuesday's presidential election. They have the look of patients awaiting the result of hospital "tests," steeling themselves for the worst, hardly daring to hope for the best. On the dot of 5 PM Eastern Time, they race to the *Washington Post* Web site to check the daily tracking poll. If Kerry's down a point (he was on Friday) the certainty hardens: we're in for it. It's not as if the prospect of a Kerry presidency betokened the dawn of a new age of sweetness and light: the best that can be said of Kerry's stated positions on the war on Iraq and the "war on terror" is that at least he treats them as two different wars. It is that the prospect of a second Bush administration inspires, among urban liberals, something close to the fear of death itself—the death of America as a civilized and civilizing presence in the world. It is that heartfelt. More than any other election in recent history, this one has become a referendum on what it means to be American, and half of the country detests the idea of living in the other half's America.

In Bush vs. Kerry, two powerful national traditions are in conflict: idealism and realism, with zealous Platonists in the White House and messy, long-winded Aristotelians in the Kerry camp. For the past two weeks, the realists have been choking on a remark made by a

Bush aide to Ron Suskind, the author of a revelatory piece about the administration that was published in *The New York Times Magazine* on October 17:

> The aide said that guys like me [Suskind] were "in what we call the reality-based community," which he defined as people who "believe that solutions emerge from your judicious study of discernible reality." I nodded and murmured something about enlightenment principles and empiricism. He cut me off. "That's not the way the world really works any more," he continued. "We're an empire now, and when we act, we create our own reality. And while you're studying that reality—judiciously, as you will—we'll act again, creating other new realities, which you can study too, and that's how things will sort out...."

The unnamed aide would have made Plato proud. The "created reality," painted in primary colors and broad brushstrokes by the Bush administration, looks like a nice place to be: freedom and democracy are on the march in Iraq; terrorists are being fought abroad so they cannot harm us at home; everyone's happy with their tax cuts; global warming is a left-wing myth; each month sees a flood of new jobs; the US is in the safe hands of a strong and resolute leader.

To quibblesome Aristotelians, every statement is an audacious lie. The occupation of Iraq is a catastrophe that grows worse by the day, and has turned the country into a breeding ground for Islamist terrorism. The security of the homeland has been dangerously neglected, except insofar as it has provided opportunities to infringe on civil liberties and turn America into a surveillance society. The tax cuts in effect make the poor subsidize the lives of the extremely rich. Environmental policy is being written by the CEOs of the energy corporations. Bush is the first president since Herbert Hoover to end an administration with fewer net jobs than existed when he came to office. The strong leader is merely the amiable front man for a gang of hard-right ideologues, both secular and religious.

There's no negotiation between the two positions. Each cancels the other. You cannot live in both worlds. Yet realists labor under the benign illusion that facts will out, that if you expose a created reality to the corrosive drip of hard news it will eventually rust away. So for the past year and more—since the fiery rationalist Howard Dean took his campaign on the road—Democrats have relied on events to prove their case for them and to destroy the blithe fiction of the God's-in-his-heaven-all's-right-with-the-world rhetoric of the administration. There's been no shortage of events—the spread of the hydra-headed Iraqi resistance, the bloody kidnap-murders, the obscenity of Abu Ghraib, the mounting death toll of American soldiers, the sham of "sovereignty." This last week alone has seen the scandal of unguarded explosives at al-Qaqa'a, the FBI investigation into Halliburton's shady dealings with the Pentagon, Ramadi's descent into chaos, the reemergence on video of Osama bin Laden looking like the cat that ate the cream, and the report suggesting that 100,000 Iraqi civilians —and not 13,000, as previously estimated—have died as a result of the invasion and occupation. Yet the polls have hardly budged—and, if anything, they've budged in Bush's favor.

Democrats despair. Believing as they do in the power of empirical evidence to change electoral opinion, they feel they should be looking not at a likely tie, to be fought through the courts for weeks and maybe months after Tuesday's election, but at a landslide triggered by the—to them—self-evident and catastrophic failure of the Bush presidency. Some of this discrepancy has to be blamed on the candidate: John Kerry's style of sonorous gravity, his lofty patrician airs, his fluency in French, his otiose qualifications and dependent clauses grate badly on an electorate accustomed to the easy demotic manners of Reagan, Clinton, and George W. Bush. He bores even his supporters. He certainly bores me.

But the poll numbers testify far more to Bush's strength than to Kerry's weakness. Bush, as he tirelessly reminds his listeners, has something more to offer than mere facts: he has "faith," "conscience," "vision," "consistency," he has "convictions" that are "steady and true." "You know what I believe," he likes to say. "A President cannot blow in the wind. A President has to make tough decisions and stand by them." (These quotes are from a speech he gave on Thursday in Saginaw, Michigan.) Such keywords and phrases play well with the Republican base of Christian fundamentalists, but they have an even more important secular application. A "created reality," like a novel, depends above all on its internal consistency, and as Plato recommended to his philosopher-kings in the *Republic*, the ideal state is necessarily dependent on a framework of "noble fictions" or "useful lies." No one is likely to mistake Bush for a philosopher-king, but he's adept at spinning watertight noble fictions to explain and justify the policies of his administration to a public that believes in faith, conscience, vision, and consistency more than it believes in untidy and time-consuming realism. And policies like the Wolfowitz plan for the forced democratization of the Middle East owe a lot more to Plato (by way of his disciple Leo Strauss at the University of Chicago) than they do to Jesus. What Bush articulates on the stump is a vision of a created reality so nearly seamless and so internally coherent that it effectively displaces and supplants the unpleasant netherworld inhabited by his Democratic opponent. All Kerry can do in response is produce a litany of what Bush trivializes as his "complaints"—and Americans tend to take a dim view of complainers.

"Human kind," wrote T. S. Eliot in "Burnt Norton," "cannot bear very much reality," and around 50 percent of voters would understandably prefer to live inside Bush's noble Platonic fiction than in Kerry's work of low mimetic realism. We've been here before. Mark Twain liked to blame the Southern Confederacy on its peculiar addiction to the romances of Sir Walter Scott: the South was lost in a storybook dream of its own aristocracy, regarding the industrial North as a base, money-grubbing, profane society, bereft of the high ideals that sustained the Southern slaveowners. The Mason-Dixon Line is drawn differently now—it pits the unbelieving cities against the God-fearing countryside and outer suburbs—but the essence of the division remains. Who's for romance? Who's for realism? Who goes with God and Plato, who with crabbed and skeptical Aristotle?

We may, if we're lucky and avoid the bogs and sloughs of long-drawn-out electoral litigation, get an answer late on Tuesday (breakfast time on Wednesday for you). In the meanwhile, it's 2 PM Pacific, 5 PM Eastern, just time enough to check the latest tracking poll before my deadline...and it's as I feared—Bush up a point at 50, Kerry down one at 47. As we go into the weekend, the creators of reality have the edge on the reporters of reality—the hapless messengers who get shot for bearing bad news. One can only pray that on Monday morning sobriety will return, and, with it, a regard for the grim facts of the case—and that the chastened mood will last through Tuesday. Fingers crossed.

—November 2004

14

TOWN VS. COUNTRY

IN 1860, A CONSERVATIVE agrarian society was in militant rebellion against an urban industrial one: watching the election returns last November 2, it was tempting to see an image, distorted but clearly recognizable, of the Civil War, as city after city went for Kerry, the countryside was solidly for Bush, and the suburbs, especially the outer suburbs, tipped the balance in favor of the Republicans. It wasn't "red states" against "blue states" so much as flaming red rural areas rising up against the big cities, and it was happening all over the country, on the supposedly liberal coasts as well as in the supposedly conservative heartland.

Seattle—secular, lefty, latte-drinking, gay-bar-laden, antiwar, Prius-driving, civically smug Seattle—is as entrenchedly blue a city as one can find this side of the Hudson. Yet even within King County, which includes Seattle but frays out on its eastern side into farmland, fir plantations, small, squelchy, *Twin Peaks*–like towns (much of David Lynch's series was shot in the county), and mountainous near-wilderness, you can see the terms on which the war is being fought on a national scale: the bitter antipathy between urbanites and ruralists, the extravagant mythmaking on both sides, the pitched battles—many of them superficially religious in character—and the damage inflicted on the American polity by the conflict. The angry red heartland isn't a distant region, quartered around the banks of the Mississippi, it's a twenty-minute drive from the steepling condos of downtown Seattle.

The urbanites, of course, dearly love the countryside (which they call the environment). Each weekend, they fan out across it, weirdly clad in the latest Velcro-fastening sports gear, looking like mobile versions of the ads in *Outside* magazine, to raft down and fly-fish in its rivers, ski its slopes, climb its rocks, hike and mountain-bike its trails, watch its wildlife, inhale its valuable air. They're known, by the countryside's inhabitants, as "206ers," after Seattle's area code. To the people who live and work in the environment, the 206ers are much more than a nuisance to be borne and a considerable source of rural revenue: they represent a force of intolerable political oppression.

Washington is a state where the city can usually narrowly outvote the countryside, as it did in 2000, when our present junior senator, Maria Cantwell, a Seattle-based Democrat who funded her own campaign with a fortune speedily acquired during the dot-com boom when she worked at RealNetworks, beat Slade Gorton, the three-term Republican incumbent, by a cigarette-paper-thin majority. She carried just five of the thirty-nine counties in the state, all in urban western Washington. During the campaign, Cantwell was painted by Gorton surrogates as a typical big-city elitist; a 206er who preferred salmon and spotted owls to people; a ruthless and uncaring enemy of the timber industry, the farmers, the mining interests (Gorton's support for a cyanide-leach gold mine in rural Okanogan County was a touchstone issue), the building trade, and anyone who chose to live and work in the environment instead of treating it as a weekend playground. Her narrow win was bemoaned as a grievous example of the tyranny of the city over the countryside, the unreasonable ability of five counties to outvote the other thirty-four, and of the bloated metropolitan leisure class over hardworking ordinary Americans of the kind who don't call AAA when they need to change a tire.

Much the same demographic pattern applies in King County itself, where metropolitan Seattle occupies less than a third of the county's total area, but can crush rural voters with its sheer density of population. So the city decides what people in the countryside may do with their land, and the county courthouse in Seattle is regularly encircled by wrathful wagon trains of horse trucks and pickups adorned with signs protesting the "Sovietization" of rural America. A couple of years ago, Ron Sims, the King County executive, issued a moratorium on building new churches (along with schools) in the "environmentally sensitive" eastern part of the county on the grounds that a church is a "large footprint item," bringing heavy traffic and other urban ills to the delicate countryside: as far as many easterners were concerned, he might as well have declared atheism as the county's official religion. Sims eventually climbed down on that one, but a string of "critical areas ordinances" has issued from his office, extending "setbacks" around streams and wetlands, and forbidding the cutting of brush and timber on as much as 65 percent of a rural property to maintain habitat and protect watersheds. Each ordinance, justified by the findings of "best available science," has brought forth howls of rage from the country dwellers, who like to claim that only those who live on the land truly understand the land, and that cargo-panted, condo-dwelling bureaucrats are arrogantly abusing their constitutional rights. "Best available science" has come to mean a catchall license to trespass, lecture, and dictate, bringing science itself under a cloud of deep rural animus and suspicion of being yet another of those legendary vices that are practiced in the city.

As the suburbs spread, and former logging towns turn into dormitories for city workers, the people who live in these "critical areas" resemble less and less the stereotype of the muddy-booted reactionary countryman. Take the not-so-hypothetical case of the young Microsoft retiree who bought a few acres in eastern King County to realize her childhood dream of having a horse farm and riding school, only to discover that land-use ordinances confined her to a clearance of 35 percent of the property, plus hundred-yard setbacks around the edge of her stream and her patch of wetland: nothing could be better calculated to convert a lifelong liberal Democrat into an angry overnight Republican. The lash of urban enlightenment over rural ignorance falls on many such backs now.

A decade ago, the easterners attempted the classic American maneuver of secession. Armed with a petition signed by 30,000 people, they sought a divorce from King County and independent status as a new entity, Cedar County. After five years of legal to-ing and fro-ing, the secessionists were defeated by a unanimous ruling from the state supreme court. "They took a chain saw to us," the chairwoman of the Cedar County movement told *The Seattle Times*, in a turn of phrase both apt and ironic in view of the chain saw's crucial symbolism in the urban–rural war. It hardly needs saying that supreme court justices tend to be big-city types: of the nine justices who make up the current Washington supreme court, seven are from the urban corridor in western Washington, one from the city of Spokane in the east, and one from Clallam County on the Olympic Peninsula, which was among the five counties carried by Maria Cantwell in her Senate race. So once again, as the secessionists saw it, the city drubbed the countryside with its imperious rule.

The rage is all the greater because the countryside knows in its heart that it is right. America's sustaining myths are rural ones: virtue resides in the soil, in the little house on the prairie, the lonely clapboard church, the one-room school, the small self-governing Puritan township. American writers, from Fenimore Cooper and Thoreau to Gary Snyder and Barry Lopez, have expended much eloquence on the theme that true wisdom is to be found in the woods, not in the arid intellectualism (read "best available science") of the city. Like Britain (and unlike France or Italy) the US, despite producing at least two of the great cities of the world, is prone to see the city, as William Cobbett saw

London, as a "great wen," a pustular, abnormal swelling on the fair face of the countryside. The modern suburban dream of *rus in urbe* reflects that feeling: to live in Issaquah, a suburban town seventeen miles east of Seattle, on the edge of the Tiger Mountain State Forest, is to conjoin oneself to the good countryside and escape the bad city. So it's hardly surprising that when the suburbs have to choose a side in the war at election time, they tend to declare themselves for the country and the mystical values that come with being so close to the smell of the woods and the footprints of the mountain lion. Suburbanites love to think that their God's little acre of tract housing is almost, if not quite, a farm (one of the most hallowed words in American mythology), and if farmers' property rights are threatened by the city, they'll go with the farmers every time.

Faced by this rebellion, the city has been quick to turn with venom on the countryside. I've heard Seattleites describe driving the few hundred miles to Spokane or Boise, Idaho, as if they had traveled through, say, Romania under the Ceauşescu dictatorship. They extol the grandeur of the environment along the route, even as they deplore the meanness of the people they saw there: their massed ranks of belligerent American flags, their forests of Bush-Cheney signs, their unspeakable restaurants, the scarifying messages on the signboards of their fundamentalist churches. From behind the steering wheel, they've seen bigots, creationists, rabid pro-lifers, environmental vandals—unwashed, illiberal America, red in tooth, claw, religion, and politics. "East of the mountains," as Seattle likes to say, meaning the Cascade Range, lies a benighted foreign country, the "Jesusland" that stole the 2004 presidential election, according to the e-mailed map of the "United States of Canada" that went the liberal rounds in early November last year.

I've been guilty of this myself. Driving one night through eastern Washington long ago, I happened to pick up an AM station on which a deep-voiced preacher was performing phone-in exorcisms, bringing sobbing women to what sounded like orgasms, as he wrestled evil spirits from their innermost beings. For a while, this curious show so colored my view of "east of the mountains" that I readily fell in with the received urban wisdom that the eastern half of the state is populated by far-right religious loonies.

Not true at all. The American Religion Data Archive (www.thearda .com), maintained by the sociology department at Pennsylvania State University, maps the whole of the United States, county by county, in terms of its religious affiliations and church membership. In states like Alabama and Arkansas, for instance, you can see the overwhelming preponderance of "Evangelical Protestant" over all other categories, including "Unclaimed," the category that includes unbelievers like me, along, I imagine, with people whose beliefs are so eccentric that they defy categorization altogether. It turns out that ungodly Seattle and King County have a lower proportion of Unclaimeds (62.7 percent) than rural counties east of the mountains such as Grant (67.8 percent), Stevens (72.7 percent), or Pend Oreille (76.6 percent). As the figure for Spokane County (63.9 percent) confirms, people in the cities are rather more likely to go to church than people in the countryside, in generally irreligious Washington.

Yet it's true that the rural east does vote in step with the Christian right—not because it's full of born-againers but because, perhaps, there is a natural coincidence of interest between the country dwellers and the evangelicals. The fundamentalists are skeptical of science; so, for its own reasons, is the countryside. Fundamentalist theology, with its elevation of personal responsibility (to your god, for your own soul, and your own property) above the merely communal, chimes very nicely with the country's view of things. American Protestantism and American individualism have been twinned since the Puritans first set up the Massachusetts Bay Colony, but in recent years the city, with its loathed science and loathed bureaucracy, has come to be perceived, in the suburbs hardly less than in the countryside, as the enemy of individualism—not for philosophical or religious reasons, but because of setbacks, and brush cutting, and dredging, and building on "critical areas."

Liberals blamed the result of the last election on "culture wars" of the kind described brilliantly by Thomas Frank in *What's the Matter with Kansas?*[1] But what's the matter with Kansas is what's the matter with Connecticut, and California, and Washington State: the countryside is up in arms against the city over the issue of land use and property rights, and the city, in its high-minded high-handedness, must bear much of the blame for this.

The hated Ron Sims acknowledged as much after the Cedar County secessionists lost their case in the state supreme court. As *The Seattle Times* reported:

> King County Executive Ron Sims today said the movement succeeded in telling the county it needs to decentralize and be more sensitive to rural concerns. "It has been a message that has clearly been received by me," Sims said.[2]

Seven years on, Sims is still in place, and the country is still coming to town, waving placards that say RON SIMS, KISS MY GRASS. One recent aggrieved protester asked a *Seattle Times* reporter, "Can I come take 65 percent of your condo?"

Late last November, the Bush administration proposed to cut around 80 percent of designated "critical habitat" for Pacific salmon and steelhead from Southern California to the Canadian border. Coming so soon after the election, the proposal looked like an extravagant thank-you note to the builders, loggers, and private landowners

---

1. *What's the Matter with Kansas?: How Conservatives Won the Heart of America* (Metropolitan Books, 2004).

2. February 5, 1998.

of the coastal heartland, and a cheerful fuck-you to the effete city crowd of environmentalists and recreational users of the countryside. Grandly scorning best available science, it gave notice to America that this administration means to champion your right to do what you damn well please on your own damn land.

It is the duty of "Civil Governments" to "protect the rights of property, as well as those of life and liberty," Isham Harris, governor of Tennessee, told the state legislature in January 1861, as he severed Tennessee from the Union. The war between the states began as a quarrel over property rights. Be grateful for small mercies: in the present rancorous division of the US, at least property means property, not slaves.

—January 2005

15

TERROR WARRIORS

IN HIS NOVEMBER 3 victory speech, President Bush, sounding the keynote of his second administration, pledged to "fight this war on terror with every resource of our national power." By saying "this" rather than "the" Bush stressed the palpable, near-at-hand quality of the war whose symbols have grown to surround us in the last three years—the tilted barrels of security cameras, BioWatch pathogen sniffers, and all the rest of the technology of security and surveillance that Matthew Brzezinski somewhat overexcitedly details in *Fortress America.*[1] Voters, at least, have been impressed. Responding to the exit pollers' question "Which ONE issue mattered most in deciding how you voted for president?," 32 percent of Bush supporters named "terrorism" (as against 5 percent of Kerry supporters), 85 percent of Bush supporters said that the country was "safer from terrorism" in 2004 than it was in 2000, and 79 percent said that the war in Iraq "has improved the long-term security of the United States." Bush's successful conflation of security at home and military aggression abroad, his insistence that Iraq "is the central front of the war on terror," was the bravura rhetorical gambit that drove much of his electoral strategy.

---

1. *Fortress America: On the Front Line of Homeland Security—An Inside Look at the Coming Surveillance State* (Bantam, 2004).

If you live, as I do, in an American city designated as a likely target by the Department of Homeland Security, the sheer proliferation of security apparatus in the streets assures you that there is a war on. Yet the nature and conduct of that war, and the character—and very existence—of our enemy, remain infuriatingly obscure: not because there's any shortage of information, or apparent information, but because so much of it has turned out to be creative guesswork or empty propaganda.

To begin with, it wasn't a war. In the immediate aftermath of September 11, the attacks were spoken of, like the 1993 bombing of the World Trade Center or the bombing of the Alfred P. Murrah Federal Building in Oklahoma City in 1995, as acts of criminal atrocity for which those who were responsible could, the President said, "be brought to justice." But within nine days the war was under way. At the joint session of Congress on September 20, Bush described it as a new brand of war, "unlike any other we have ever known," of "covert operations, secret even in success." In Dick Cheney's words, it was to be fought "in the shadows: this is a mean, nasty, dangerous, dirty business. We have to operate in that arena."

Bush and Cheney were introducing the general public to the idea of asymmetric or "fourth-generation" warfare, involving a nation-state in conflict with a "non-state actor," whose basic outlines were nicely described by William S. Lind and four Army and Marine Corps officers in an article published in the *Marine Corps Gazette*.[2] Lind et al. wrote:

> In broad terms, fourth generation warfare seems likely to be widely dispersed and largely undefined; the distinction between war and peace will be blurred to the vanishing point. It will be nonlinear, possibly to the point of having no definable battlefields

---

2. "The Changing Face of War: Into the Fourth Generation" (October 1989), pp. 22–26.

or fronts. The distinction between "civilian" and "military" may disappear. Actions will occur concurrently throughout all participants' depth, including their society as a cultural, not just a physical, entity.

Major military facilities, such as airfields, fixed communications sites, and large headquarters will become rarities because of their vulnerability; the same may be true of civilian equivalents, such as seats of government, power plants, and industrial sites (including knowledge as well as manufacturing industries). Success will depend heavily on effectiveness in joint operations as lines between responsibility and mission become very blurred.

The first four sentences quoted above seem as smart a description as any I've read of the peculiar situation we find ourselves in at present —a world of chronic blur, full of newly slippery words that mean something different from what they meant before September 2001. Just as John Ashcroft's scheme for Operation TIPS (short for Terrorism Information and Prevention System) raised the question of whether one should treat the neighborhood mailman as a fellow civilian or a pfc. in military intelligence, so the texture of ordinary life and talk has taken on a disturbingly ambiguous quality, to the point where peace wears the face of war, and war dissimulates as peace. As Admiral Fitzwallace (John Amos), the fictional chairman of the Joint Chiefs on *The West Wing*, admitted to the White House chief of staff in an episode of the series broadcast in 2002, "I can't tell when it's peacetime and wartime anymore."

In Cheney's "arena" of shadows, one needs to be as suspicious of unattended language as of any other form of baggage. The phrase "war on terror" is a case in point. To isolate it in skeptical quotation marks can be an act of mild, justifiable pedantry: terrorism is a belligerent means, not an object or an enemy, and declaring war on it is like declaring war on tanks, or bows and arrows. It can also be an act of political dissent, identifying the writer's mistrust of the whole enterprise; and the reverse is true. A puzzling feature of Michael Ignatieff's *The Lesser Evil*, for instance, is its repeated refusal to flag the phrase with quotes: "The norms that govern a war on terror are not the monopoly of government.... Standards for a war on terror will be set by adversarial moral competition.... A democratic war on terror needs to subject all coercive measures to *the dignity test....*"[3] In a book otherwise dedicated to the scrupulous examination of conventional assumptions, one outsized, unexamined assumption squats at the center like the elephant in the living room and opens Ignatieff to the charge that he's not so much a disinterested critic of the terror warriors as their in-house philosopher.

But Ignatieff may be right. When so many basic notions, like security, war, enemy, network, chatter, threat, totalitarian, are infected with new and dubious meanings, there's a temptation to reach continually for quotation marks as if they were pairs of rubber gloves. Better to remember Lind and his colleagues: fourth-generation warfare is altering the language in ways that we must learn to live with.

The war on terror has brought back the sap of youth to the veins of old cold warriors, like Richard Pipes, the historian of Russia, leader of Team B, and staff member of the National Security Council in the Reagan years, who seized on the Beslan school massacre in September 2004 to make a vital distinction. In an Op-Ed piece for *The New York Times* Pipes wrote:

> The attacks on New York and the Pentagon were unprovoked and had no specific objective. Rather, they were part of a general assault of Islamic extremists bent on destroying non-Islamic civilizations. As such, America's war with Al Qaeda is

---

3. *The Lesser Evil: Political Ethics in an Age of Terror* (Princeton University Press, 2004).

non-negotiable. But the Chechens do not seek to destroy Russia
—thus there is always an opportunity for compromise.[4]

Pipes advised Vladimir Putin to hasten to the negotiating table, parlay
with the Chechen rebels, and spare Russia further attacks. It's axiomatic to America's war on terror, as Pipes makes plain, that our enemy
—variously known as Islamofascism, Islamist extremism, global
jihad—has no rational agenda beyond its desire to destroy the United
States out of remorseless, theologically inspired hatred for its values.

To justify their case, Pipes and his kind treat as beneath their notice
the shopping list of causes and demands presented by Osama bin
Laden, Ayman al-Zawahiri, and others in their February 1998 declaration of "Jihad against Jews and Crusaders," which is every bit as
specific as the complaints of the Chechen rebels. There's no mention
of American values in bin Laden's call for the removal of US bases
from Saudi Arabia (a demand that has since been quietly met) and
for an end to "the Americans' continuing aggression against the Iraqi
people using the Peninsula as a staging post," or in his indictment of
the American "endeavor to fragment all the states of the region
such as Iraq, Saudi Arabia, Egypt, and Sudan into paper statelets and
through their disunion and weakness to guarantee Israel's survival
and the continuation of the brutal crusade occupation of the Peninsula."[5] To fight Richard Pipes's war on terror, one has to take it as
read that the Islamists' seeming preoccupation with affairs in the Arab
world is merely a smokescreen to cover their pathological loathing of
the United States—which could be true, but it'd be nice to see it
argued in the open air and not in invisible ink.

The most rousing call to arms has come from Norman Podhoretz
in an enormous article in *Commentary* titled "World War IV: How It

---

4. "Give the Chechens a Land of Their Own," *The New York Times*, September 9, 2004.

5. See www.fas.org/irp/world/para/docs/980223-fatwa.htm.

Started, What It Means, and Why We Have to Win."[6] Here, in passing, he nicely disposes of the question whether America's unconditional support for Israel plays any serious part in the global jihadists' thinking. "Hatred of Israel," Podhoretz explains, is "a surrogate for anti-Americanism, rather than the reverse." "If the Jewish state had never come into existence, the United States would still have stood as an embodiment of everything that most of these Arabs considered evil." For Podhoretz, as for Pipes, it's essential to get rid of the idea that Islamist extremism might spring from causes and concerns within the Middle East, and to insist that the enemy's quarrel is not with America's policies but with the fact of America in and of itself:

> His objective is not merely to murder as many of us as possible and to conquer our land. Like the Nazis and Communists before him, he is dedicated to the destruction of everything good for which America stands.

Or, as the subterranean monster, the Underminer, announces in the closing frames of *The Incredibles*, "I declare war on Peace and Happiness."

With Israel conveniently out of the picture, Podhoretz addresses his mighty theme—the nobility of the Bush Doctrine as it confronts the third great totalitarian power of modern times. The hot war against Nazi Germany and the Axis powers and the cold war against Soviet Russia were foreshadowing preludes to the war now in progress, in which George W. Bush, "a passionate democratic idealist of the Reaganite stamp," has heroically personified "a repudiation of moral relativism and an entirely unapologetic assertion of the need for and the possibility of moral judgment in the realm of world affairs," thereby restoring America to its pay-any-price-bear-any-burden internationalist and democratic roots.

Despite Podhoretz's ample retrospective catalog of injuries and

---

6. *Commentary*, September 2004, pp. 17–54.

humiliations inflicted on the United States by various Muslim groups and individuals (including the PLO, the PFLP, the Tehran students in 1979, Hezbollah, Abu Abbas, Abu Nidal, and al-Qaeda), it's hard to see how the many people who committed these acts share a single theology, let alone represent a unified totalitarian force comparable with Nazism or Soviet communism. When Podhoretz giddily announces that a major goal of the war on terror must be "the reform and modernization of the Islamic religion itself," one is sharply reminded that nothing in his essay suggests any serious familiarity with the religion to which he so breezily appoints himself as the new Calvin or Luther.

In his envoi, "History's Call," Podhoretz quotes George F. Kennan, writing in 1947 to welcome the cold war as a challenge sent by Providence to test America's national mettle. Adapting Kennan, Podhoretz says:

> Now "our entire security as a nation"—including, to a greater extent than in 1947, our physical security—once more depends on whether we are ready and willing to accept and act upon the responsibilities of moral and political leadership that history has yet again so squarely placed upon our shoulders. Are we ready? Are we willing?

The gallant tone and dramatic historical sweep of the piece are calculated to make a fellow proud, as Tom Lehrer once sang, to be a soldier, but the questions of just how and where this inspiring war is to be fought, and against precisely whom, grow increasingly opaque as Podhoretz works his way through some 35,000 words of martial uplift. He spends so much of his time energetically putting to the sword paleoconservatives (anti-Semites to a man), and fainthearted, détente-addicted Democrats and their lackeys in the press and in Europe that one tends to lose sight altogether of the ill-assorted band of Muslims—Palestinians, Syrians, Iranians, and, of course, Osama bin Laden and al-Qaeda—who, presumably, constitute an even graver threat to the US than the combined forces of Michael Moore, Bill Clinton, Brent Scowcroft, Pat Buchanan, Robert Novak, and *The New York Times*.

The name al-Qaeda means something different practically every time it's used. Sometimes it's a synecdoche, intended to conjure shadowy legions of all the various militant Islamist groups around the globe, which is how Podhoretz generally refers to it. Sometimes it's held to be a transnational corporation, like Starbucks, with a spiderweb of sleeper-cell outlets spread worldwide, but controlled from a headquarters somewhere in Pakistan or Afghanistan. Sometimes it's described as a franchise outfit, like 7-Eleven, renting out its name to any small-time independent shopkeeper who's prepared to subscribe to the company program, and sometimes as a single store, or bank, owned and operated by Osama bin Laden.

This fogginess has been thickened by the political and journalistic habit of using speculative—often wildly speculative—conjunctions to connect particular people to the organization. Terrorist suspects, along with almost anyone temporarily detained under the provisions of the Patriot Act, are said to have alleged ties to, be associated with, or be linked to al-Qaeda. Although most of these associations have subsequently proved to be fictitious (as in the case of Brandon Mayfield, the unfortunate Portland, Oregon, lawyer who was arrested by the FBI for his supposed involvement in the Madrid train bombing), the impression is left that members of al-Qaeda are strewn as thickly over the ground, and in our very midst, as those of the AARP.

Although the interrogation of some captured key figures with proven connections to bin Laden (among them Khalid Sheikh Mohammed, Ramzi Binalshibh, and Ramzi Yousef) has produced a great deal of detailed intelligence about past plots, as *The 9/11 Commission Report*[7]

---

7. *The 9/11 Commission Report: Final Report of the National Commission on Terrorist Attacks upon the United States* (Norton, 2004).

abundantly testifies, it doesn't seem—so far as one can judge from what has been made public—to have revealed much about the organization and structure of al-Qaeda itself, which remains as nebulous as ever.

The prevailing view of what al-Qaeda is and does is plausibly and succinctly put by Richard A. Clarke in *Against All Enemies*.[8] Working from intelligence available to him when he was counterterrorism czar for both the Clinton and George W. Bush administrations, Clarke, connecting every dot (even such faint ones as those that might link Terry Nichols, the Oklahoma City bomber, with Ramzi Yousef and/ or Khalid Sheikh Mohammed), pieces together a fearsome but limited picture of the organization that he calls "a worldwide political conspiracy masquerading as a religious sect." Interestingly, the picture—though it has gained many more contingent details—differs very little from the one sketched in the spring of 1996, when Jamal al-Fadl, who had embezzled money from bin Laden's entourage in Sudan and was in fear of his life, defected to the Americans. According to Clarke, al-Fadl told his interrogators that al-Qaeda was a

> network . . . widespread and active, with a presence through affiliate groups and sleeper cells in over fifty countries. Ramzi Yousef and the blind sheikh [Omar Abdel Rahman] had been part of it. Bin Laden was not just its financier, he was its mastermind.

The most revealing moment in *Against All Enemies* comes near the end, when Clarke is about to shift from his National Security Council job to become presidential adviser on cyberspace security, and his deputy, Roger Cressey, accuses him of reluctance to make the move:

---

8. *Against All Enemies: Inside America's War on Terror* (Free Press, 2004).

"You're not gonna move now, are you? Finally, they're paying attention to yah, so you wanna hang around and get your White Whale, huh?" Cressey had grown up near the fish piers in Gloucester, Massachusetts. He knew about obsessive fishing boat captains.

At the NSC, Clarke as he tells it was desperate to persuade successive administrations of the overwhelming importance of al-Qaeda (and, after September 11, of the perilous irrelevance of the proposed invasion of Iraq). Al-Qaeda was his professional baby, his idée fixe, and his grievance, to be nursed in defiance of such uncomprehending skeptics and know-nothings as Paul Wolfowitz and Condoleezza Rice ("As I briefed Rice on al-Qaeda, her facial expression gave me the impression that she had never heard the term before"). Only Clarke understood the paramount need to focus on the pursuit of Moby-Dick. As Melville wrote:

> The White Whale swam before him as the monomaniac incarnation of all those malicious agencies which some deep men feel eating in them, till they are left living on with half a heart and half a lung.... All that most maddens and torments; all that stirs up the lees of things; all truth with malice in it ... all evil, to crazy Ahab, were visibly personified, and made practically assailable in Moby Dick.

The 9/11 Commission plainly recognized Clarke's kinship with Melville's captain:

> Clarke hoped that the August 1998 missile strikes would mark the beginning of a sustained campaign against Bin Ladin. Clarke was, as he later admitted, "obsessed" with Bin Ladin, and the embassy bombings gave him new scope for pursuing his obsession.

Terrorism had moved high up among the President's concerns, and Clarke's position had elevated accordingly.

Yet the commission's description of al-Qaeda closely echoes that of Clarke, whose name is footnoted countless times in the report. Though the authors acknowledge that they were dealing with a crazy Ahab, their own version of bin Laden's organization is in very large part Ahab's not-altogether-reliable account of the nature and significance of the white whale.

Michael Scheuer, formerly Anonymous, the author of *Imperial Hubris*,[9] is another raging Ahab, but as a CIA analyst and not a White House aide, Scheuer has been able to range more widely, and with greater intellectual dispassion, than Clarke. His white whale is not al-Qaeda but the Bush administration and his own agency bosses, against whom his book is leveled like a harpoon in one long, furious, ironic tirade. His fascination with Osama bin Laden verges almost on hero worship as he extols bin Laden's brilliance, eloquence, sanity, religious sincerity, acute tactical skills, and the essential reasonableness of his campaign of "defensive jihad."[10] Scheuer's message, repeated many times in different forms, is best summed up near the end of *Imperial Hubris*:

The United States is hated across the Islamic world because of specific US government policies and actions. That hatred is concrete not abstract, martial not intellectual, and it will grow

---

9. *Imperial Hubris: Why the West Is Losing the War On Terror* (Brassey's, 2004).

10. For example, in the exchange between Scheuer and Tim Russert on NBC's *Meet the Press*, November 21, 2004:

Mr. Scheuer: [Osama bin Laden] is really a remarkable man, a great man in many ways, without the connotation positive or negative. He's changed the course of history. You just have to try to take your fourth-grader's class to the White House visitors' center...

Mr. Russert: When you say "great man," people cringe.

Mr. Scheuer: Yes, sir. Absolutely they cringe, but a great man is someone—a great individual

for the foreseeable future.... America is hated and attacked because Muslims believe they know precisely what the United States is doing in the Islamic world. They know partly because of bin Laden's words, partly because of satellite television, but mostly because of the tangible reality of US policy. We are at war with an al Qaeda–led, worldwide Islamist insurgency because of and to defend those policies, and not, as President Bush has mistakenly said, "to defend freedom and all that is good and just in the world."

Scheuer warns of huge body counts on both sides that "will include as many or more civilians as combatants," "a Sherman-like razing of infrastructure," land mines to seal borders and passes, "displaced populations, and refugee flows." "This sort of bloody-mindedness is neither admirable nor desirable, but it will remain America's only option so long as she stands by her failed policies toward the Muslim world."

Scheuer's al-Qaeda is more frightening than the versions offered by ideologues like Norman Podhoretz or by dot-connecting terrorist hunters like Richard Clarke because it is an entirely rational enemy, motivated by causes just as dear as those that drive Americans. It is bent, as we are here, on defending its own liberties in its homelands; it is amply armed, and is equipped with a better understanding of the strategies of fourth-generation warfare than Americans yet possess. Worse, we have no realistic knowledge of its size, its organizational

---

is someone who changes the course of history. And certainly in the last five or six years, America has changed dramatically in the way we behave, in the way we travel. Certainly he's bleeding us to death in terms of money. Look at the budget deficit now. Much of that goes against Osama bin Laden.

Mr. Russert: Do you see him as a very formidable enemy?

Mr. Scheuer: Tremendously formidable enemy, sir, an admirable man. If he was on our side, he would be dining at the White House. He would be a freedom fighter, a resistance fighter. It's—and again, that's not to praise him, but it is to say that until we take the measure of the man and the power of his words, we're very much going to be on the short end of the stick.

structure, or its plans. Scheuer recently came out of his always-thin anonymity to tell *The New York Times*: "We still don't know how big it is. We still, today, don't know the battle order of Al Qaeda."[11]

Alternatively, one might try thinking of al-Qaeda as a figment of our inflamed imaginations, a mirage conjured by a sleeper cell of neoconservative witch doctors in Washington and given suitably terrifying substance by a credulous press. This bracingly contrarian view is argued, with vigor and wit, by Adam Curtis, a well-regarded British documentary filmmaker, in a series of three one-hour programs recently aired on the BBC under the title *The Power of Nightmares*,[12] and widely discussed in the UK. Fast-moving, full of ingenious musical and cinematic puns, Curtis's series is best watched as an epic political cartoon in the manner of Daumier or Ralph Steadman. It freely bends the facts to fit its vision, it distorts, it overcolors, it grossly—and entertainingly—simplifies, yet, as only a cartoon can, it captures an aspect of its subject that has so far escaped even the most skeptical observers of the war on terror.

Chronicling the simultaneous rise of militant Islamism and American neoconservatism, Curtis represents the two movements as each other's doppelgängers, both powered by disgust with the moral degeneracy of the liberal West, each under the spell of a founding godfather. As Sayyid Qutb, the Egyptian literary critic and author of the primer of modern jihad, *Milestones*, inspired the Islamists, so Leo Strauss inspired the neoconservatives. (This view of Strauss has been convincingly deconstructed by Mark Lilla.[13]) Plato's idea of the noble

---

11. See James Risin, "Evolving Nature of Al Qaeda Is Misunderstood, Critic Says," *The New York Times*, November 8, 2004.

12. BBC Two, October 20 and 27 and November 3, 2004.

13. "Leo Strauss: The European," *The New York Review of Books*, October 21, 2004, and "The Closing of the Straussian Mind," *The New York Review of Books*, November 4, 2004.

fiction, or useful lie, is here attributed exclusively to Strauss: it was the sinister Strauss, according to Curtis, who taught the neocons how to cynically manufacture myths to persuade the American people that they were on the side of goodness in the perpetual Manichaean struggle against the all-enveloping forces of evil.

Curtis's neocons—Richard Perle, Paul Wolfowitz, the Kristols (father and son), Dick Cheney, Donald Rumsfeld, Richard Pipes, Michael Ledeen—might as well be equipped with masks, black cloaks, and vampire teeth. Assembling in the darkness of the Ford administration, the conspirators first set out to destroy Henry Kissinger, the arch-pragmatist and advocate of détente, then, with Pipes installed as leader of Team B, they vastly inflate the threat posed to the United States by Soviet Russia. They invent devastating Soviet weaponry so secret that no Western intelligence agency is yet aware of its existence; they spin into being a worldwide terror network, controlled from Moscow, in which the IRA, Black September, the Baader-Meinhof Group, the Red Brigades, and numerous others are all financed and armed by their Russian masters.

After the collapse of the Soviet Union, Curtis's neocons turn to the fabrication of domestic noble fictions, and bring down Clinton. David Brock appears on camera to confess that he was employed by the neocons, working from their *American Spectator* safe house, as a "political terrorist." So the stage is set for the neocons' most ambitious concoction, the enlargement of al-Qaeda from a small group of followers of Osama bin Laden to the vast network, threatening the survival of Western civilization, as portrayed by Podhoretz, Clarke, and President Bush.

In 1996, Jamal al-Fadl, the defecting Sudanese embezzler, had told his American interrogators whatever they wanted to hear. They needed a network; he gave them a network. They needed a mastermind; he gave them bin Laden. Wanting to prosecute bin Laden under US law as it related to organized crime, the Americans required a company name for bin Laden's organization: they called it al-Qaeda, or the base of operations. So, in Curtis's account, al-Qaeda began life as a US-manufactured legal fiction.

With the neocon mythmakers now in senior government positions, September 11 made it easy to cast al-Qaeda in the Evil Empire role that they had previously scripted for the Soviet Union—same global network, same central control, with a stand-in Kremlin located in the Afghan countryside. Their problem, in Curtis's view, was an almost complete lack of hard evidence. In *The Power of Nightmares*, Donald Rumsfeld, armed with an artist's diagram of a magnificent underground fortress supposedly soon to be found in the mountains of Tora Bora, is shown explaining the wonders of the place to Tim Russert on *Meet the Press*: the warren of bedrooms and offices; the ventilation, phone, and computer systems; the secret exits; the ground-floor entrances, big enough to drive fleets of tanks in and out of. Rumsfeld says, "And there are not just one of those, there are *many* of those."

But when Tora Bora is actually reached, its legendary caves turn out to be just caves; small, dark, unimproved, empty except for a few stacks of ammunition boxes.

Not long after, Bush appears, telling the nation that "we've thwarted terr'ists in Buffalo—and Seattle—Portland—Detroit—North Carolina—Tampa, Florida.... We're determined to stop the enemy before it can strike our people." But every case on Bush's coast-to-coast list of sleeper cells has either fallen to pieces in the courts or resulted in convictions on relatively trivial charges. The best evidence that the FBI could dig up consisted of such incriminating items as a tourist video of a visit to Disneyland; an e-mail from Mukhta al-Bakri, saying goodbye to his American friends because he was going to Bahrain to get married, which was held by the FBI to be a coded message announcing that al-Bakri was going to mount a suicide-bomb attack on the US Sixth Fleet; and some graceless doodles in a day-planner, made by a long-dead schizophrenic Yemeni, that were interpreted as a terrorist's map of a US air base in Turkey.[14]

Curtis argues that al-Qaeda is a "phantom enemy." Its "hidden network of terror" is an illusion assiduously fostered by politicians who, in playing on our fears of an imagined future, have cynically grasped the principle that "those with the darkest imaginations become the most powerful." The argument is well worth putting forward (and it's to be hoped that some brave American network will dare to screen *The Power of Nightmares*), but it has one crucially disabling flaw.

"There is no al-Qaeda organization," asserts one of Curtis's star witnesses, Jason Burke, author of *Al Qaeda: Casting a Shadow of Terror*,[15] in a climactic moment of the final episode—a remark that elicited admiring gasps from the tiny American audience to whom I showed the series. That may be true as far as it goes, but it does not go nearly as far as Burke himself goes in an article in the May/June 2004 issue of *Foreign Policy*, where he writes:

> Today, the structure that was built in Afghanistan has been destroyed, and bin Laden and his associates have scattered or been arrested or killed. There is no longer a central hub for Islamic militancy. But the al Qaeda worldview, or "al Qaeda-ism," is growing stronger every day. This radical internationalist ideology—sustained by anti-Western, anti-Zionist, and anti-Semitic rhetoric—has adherents among many individuals and groups, few of whom are currently linked in any substantial way to bin Laden or those around him. They merely follow

---

14. Tom Ridge, interviewed by Gwen Ifill on CNN's *Washington Week* (December 3, 2004) shortly after he resigned as secretary of the Department of Homeland Security, admitted, "...Can I tell you today, there are X number of incidents we were able to thwart and prevent? Cannot."

15. I. B. Tauris, 2004.

his precepts, models, and methods. They act in the style of al Qaeda, but they are only part of al Qaeda in the very loosest sense. That's why Israeli intelligence services now prefer the term "jihadi international" instead of "al Qaeda."

When the next major terrorist attack on the United States takes place, it will not greatly matter if the attackers turn out to have been al-Qaeda or al-Qaedaists. Bin Laden survives as an inspiring folk hero. The political causes and theological justifications for jihad are as alive as ever; in such places as the shabby storefront mosque in Harburg, the Hamburg suburb where Mohamed Atta and his colleagues found their suicidal vocation, the toxic dream of wreaking vengeance on the Great Satan will surely continue to exert its hold on the minds of well-heeled and technologically capable young men outraged by US policies and actions in the Middle East, and impassioned by religious beliefs of fresh and furious vitality. (As Max Rodenbeck wrote last April, the fiercely puritanical, Salafist strain of Islam practiced by bin Laden and his followers and competitors is a modern, reformist movement in full bloom, though the reformation is hardly what Norman Podhoretz has in mind for the religion.[16]) If these constitute a phantom, it's a remarkably close and fleshly one. Throughout the recent campaign, Abu Musab al-Zarqawi's Tawhid and Jihad Group, operating from an undiscoverable fastness somewhere in Iraq, supplied us with a string of almost inconceivably gruesome pictures of terrorism in action, as it beheaded civilian hostages, some of them Americans, on videotape.

Yet the Curtis films are persuasive in their exposure of the futility of much of the present conduct of the war on terror—the obsession with smashing imaginary networks, the pretense of fighting terrorists abroad to prevent them from attacking us at home, the notion that a

16. "Islam Confronts Its Demons," *The New York Review of Books*, April 29, 2004.

pervasive idea can be decapitated if only its mastermind can be hunted down, and the dangerous relish for promiscuous surveillance. Aided by a federal grant of $5.1 million, the city of Chicago is spending $8.6 million on a system of smart video cameras, equipped with software that will raise the alarm when the cameras spot people loitering, wandering in circles, hanging around outside public buildings, or stopping their cars on the shoulders of highways. "Anyone walking in public is liable to be almost constantly watched," reported Stephen Kinzer in *The New York Times*.[17] The Department of Homeland Security is the co-sponsor, with the FBI and the Justice Department, of Operation Predator, intended to track down pedophiles via their use of the Internet—presumably because pedophiles, whose civil liberties are held in high esteem by almost nobody, are ideal guinea pigs for a more sweeping exercise in cyberspying that might net terrorists.

If Richard Clarke's switch from the National Security Council to adviser on cyberspace security looked at first blush like a demotion, it probably wasn't: our e-mails, shared files, and visits to suspect Internet sites are obviously more likely to identify us as al-Qaedaists than any tendency we may exhibit to wander in circles in front of tall buildings. When FBI director Robert Mueller announced that Operation Predator "sends a clear message that the digital environment will not offer sanctuary to those pedophiles who lurk in peer-to-peer networks. We will identify you. We will pursue you. We will bring you to justice,"[18] it seems improbable, given the DHS's involvement in the scheme, that he had pedophiles only, or mainly, in mind.

In its present form, the war on terror is a cripplingly expensive, meagerly productive effort to locate, catch, and kill bad guys around the

---

17. "Chicago Moving to 'Smart' Surveillance Cameras," *The New York Times*, September 21, 2004.

18. Robert Mueller, May 14, 2004; see ww.fbi.gov/dojpressrel/pressrel04/p2p051404.htm.

globe. Its successes are hardly less random, or more effective in the long term, than those that might be achieved by a platoon of men armed with flyswatters entering a slaughterhouse whose refrigeration has been off for a week. The US, desperately short of Arabic speakers and translators, lacks the basic intelligence abilities needed to conduct such a threat-based, "go-to-the-source" war, as Stephen Flynn labels it in *America the Vulnerable*,[19] his brisk, cool, and hearteningly constructive account of how the Bush administration has neglected the defense of our exposed flanks in its headlong, enraged pursuit of hidden enemies.

Flynn, a former Coast Guard commander and director for global issues on the NSC staff under Clinton, effectively turns the war on terror on its head, inviting us to concentrate not on covert networks of terrorists, real or imagined, but on the vital and all too permeable networks of trade and communication that connect the US with the rest of the world. "Americans need to grow up," he writes: acts of terrorism—by al-Qaedaists and by others—are a fact of modern life, like airline disasters and car crashes, and are no more susceptible to being eradicated than crime itself. "The best we can do is to keep terrorism within manageable proportions."

He sketches a credible scenario in which four simultaneous attacks are made on the United States, involving three truck bombs and a bomb in a shipping container, in Newark, Detroit, Long Beach, and Miami. Fatalities are restricted to a few motorists who are incinerated on Detroit's Ambassador Bridge, but because the bombs contain americium-241 and cesium-137 they spread panic out of all proportion to their actual damage. (Terror, not death, is the chief consequence of the much-talked-up but physically ineffective dirty bomb.) People flee the infected cities. America closes its borders, paralyzing world trade.

---

19. *America the Vulnerable: How Our Government Is Failing to Protect Us from Terrorism* (HarperCollins, 2004).

Supermarket shelves are emptying. There's talk of airlifting food to Hawaii. The social, economic, and political costs of the attacks (which in themselves cause no more harm than the average industrial accident) are beyond calculation.

America, in Flynn's description, presents itself to terrorists as an enormous sitting duck, and its democratic system is no less at risk than its bridges, ports, agriculture, and chemical plants. The administration, addicted to secrecy, alternates between treating its citizens as children who must be shielded from knowledge of the danger they are in, and as likely suspects who must be continually surveilled. Our greatest and most alarming vulnerability is not to terrorist bombs but to "self-inflicted harm to our liberties and way of life."

Risk management is Flynn's technical specialty, and much of his book is devoted to practical, cost-effective measures to strengthen and make as safe as is reasonably possible the daily flow of goods and people in and out of the United States. Track the movement of containers around the world with global positioning system transponders, and install intrusion sensors within the containers. Establish red and green lanes for cargo, as for passengers. Monitor the food supply chain with electronic tags. Such unexciting-sounding proposals (Flynn makes dozens of them) would go a long way toward making visible and open to inspection the vast circulatory system that is now largely hidden from view, and whose obscurity offers limitless possibilities to be exploited by terrorists.

Flynn argues that most of the cost of building a terrorist-deterrent system of transportation security would be willingly borne by the private sector: shipping companies would latch on to the advantages of joining the green, or fast-track, lane, and the devices they'd have to buy in order to qualify for membership would benefit them by improving inventory control as much as it would aid the national security project. Most of the necessary equipment would quickly pay for itself, and result in smoother, more rapid passage of goods than exists at present.

But Flynn's detailed plans are only the outward and visible signs of the important idea that drives his book—the conviction that American democracy can safely withstand a terrorist attack that is sensibly anticipated and prepared for but could collapse in the panic attending attacks for which the population is physically, emotionally, and intellectually entirely unprepared. In *America the Vulnerable*, it is not just the movements of American commercial goods that are vulnerable; the Bush administration has failed to safeguard the democratic system, which is its most precious and fragile charge. On one hand, it jiggers with the color-coded alert system, rigs cities with spy cameras, and speaks darkly of secret intelligence that more often than not turns out to have been no real intelligence at all. On the other, it assures us that we are safe in its hands, and that, in Flynn's words, "our marching orders as citizens are to keep shopping and traveling." Government is most to be feared when it treats its people as babies, the way the administration does now.

Flynn is no alarmist. His writing is even-toned to a fault, his manner still that of the unflappable captain on the bridge of the Coast Guard patrol ship, but his warning is explicit: if the war on terror continues to be waged in its present form, it's likely to put democracy itself in peril:

> The secretive, top-down, us-versus-them culture that is pervasive in government security circles must give way to more inclusive processes.... Rather than working assiduously to keep the details of terrorism and our vulnerabilities out of the public domain, the federal government should adopt a new imperative that recognizes that Americans have to be far better informed about the dangers that they face.... How much security is enough? We have done enough when the American people can conclude that a future attack on US soil will be an exceptional event that does not require wholesale changes to how we go

about our lives. . . . We must continue to remind the world that it is not military might that is the source of our strength but our belief that mankind can govern itself in such a way as to secure the blessings of liberty.

These are temperate, wise, and practical thoughts. What is potentially to be feared more, even, than the prospect of another major attack of September 11 proportions or worse is that, in the second Bush administration now beginning, voices like Flynn's will go unheard, while those of such intemperate terror warriors as Podhoretz and Pipes will be listened to with a respectful attention they in no way deserve.

—January 2005

16

OUR SECRET SHARERS

AT THE BEGINNING of Joseph Conrad's novel *Under Western Eyes*, the quiet and diligent student Razumov finds himself unwillingly harboring in his St. Petersburg rooms a terrorist, the "sanguinary fanatic" Haldin, who has just thrown the bomb that killed a government minister. The reader quickly comes to understand that Razumov and Haldin are doubles, each the other's alter ego, or "secret sharer," to borrow the title of another related Conrad story. As we now come to grips with the discovery of sanguinary fanatics in our own blocks of flats and neighborhoods, it's worth trying to take the Conradian line, and to explore not their barbaric alienness but their long intimacy with us, and ours with them.

It was a striking fact that the September 11 hijackers—Mohamed Atta, Ziad Jarrah, and company—learned their brand of murderous revolutionism not in the Middle East, where they grew up, but in the West, where they were students. In particular, they congregated in the polyglot suburb of Harburg, south of the river from Hamburg; a place that in its social and economic makeup looks a lot like the shabbier bits of Leeds, Yorkshire, or the London inner suburbs of Stockwell, Tulse Hill, and Streatham Hill, where the London bombers found their lodgings—that unpicturesque terrain of flats, terraced family housing, betting shops, malodorous hairdressers, ethnic groceries and restaurants, stalled traffic, broken pavements, boarded-up shop-fronts, the amiable muddle of gimcrack domestic and commercial architecture dating from the 1880s to the near present. Nowhere could be more "Western" in its style of down-at-heel free enterprise. This is the landscape of lax secular capitalism, out of which people—many of them recent immigrants—have quarried their own small communities, where indigent loners can easily find a room to let, the natural habitat of the eccentric sect or coterie. Anything goes. Pluralism reigns. When the ailing newsagent-tobacconist closes down, it might morph overnight into an adult video store, a kebab house, a shop selling tropical fish, a £1-an-hour Internet café, or the kind of improvised mini-mosque where Atta and his colleagues sat at the feet of their fire-breathing imam. Here's modern democracy, cheap and cheerful: so long as you can pay the rent, you can pretty much do and think as you please. Of the September 11 attackers, George W. Bush blandly proclaimed, "They hate us for our freedoms." The modest urban freedoms of, say, Streatham Hill, a favorite stamping ground of mine, since I usually stay two blocks west of it when I'm in London (and was saddened to see it recently come out on top in a poll to find "Britain's worst street"), are as essential and basic as any we enjoy.

Yet such freedoms—"the West" in its most everyday and palpable form—have aroused disdain and revulsion in quarters far removed from those usually associated with Salafist jihadis. In 1964, when Sayyid Qutb published *Milestones*, the primary inspirational book of the jihad movement, he drew as much on the conservative literature of the West as on the teachings of Islamic fundamentalists. Qutb, an Egyptian who achieved "martyrdom" in 1966 when he was executed by President Nasser, began his professional life as a literary scholar and teacher. For his generation of foreign students of English, the great modern poem was T. S. Eliot's *The Waste Land*, and the required reading on modern Western culture included such grim jeremiads as Oswald Spengler's *Decline of the West*, José Ortega y Gasset's *The*

Revolt of the Masses, and Arnold Toynbee's doorstopping, ten-volume *A Study of History*. Qutb's disgust with what he called "this rubbish heap of the West" (was he, I wonder, consciously trying to echo Eliot's question, central to *The Waste Land*, "What are the roots that clutch, what branches grow/Out of this stony rubbish?"?) reflected a powerful vein of Western literary thinking. The West was morally bankrupt and degenerate. Mass democracy was in the process of destroying the order on which a healthy civilization depends. Profane, insolent, chaotic, lost to its own history and culture, the Christian West was rotting from within and going the way of the ruined civilizations of the past, from the Minoans to the Romans. As Eliot wrote, in lines that kept on running through my mind on the morning of September 11, 2001:

> *Falling towers*
> *Jerusalem Athens Alexandria*
> *Vienna London*
> *Unreal*

Qutb's peculiar genius was to make a combustible link between such a very Western, pessimistic, and apocalyptic vision of the West's decline with the specifically Islamic notion of *jahiliyyah*—the condition of ignorance, selfishness, depravity, and godlessness that existed in Arabia before the saving arrival of the Prophet Muhammad. Adroitly collapsing the twentieth into the seventh century, he found in modern America (where he spent two lonely years, filled with contempt for what he saw there) the same state of repulsive *jahiliyyah* from which the Arabs had been rescued by divine revelation in the shape of the Koran. Up to this point, Qutb's thinking remained in tune with that of many Western literary modernists: Eliot and Spengler, one feels, might have relished the *jahiliyyah* analogy as an interesting Arab response to their work. But to his cross-cultural musings, Qutb added the toxin of a romantic call to arms. Faced with the waste land, or rubbish heap, he called on his readers to destroy it: "Either Islam will remain, or Jayilliyah: Islam cannot agree to a situation which is half-Islam or half-Jayilliyah." In a long abstruse chapter, "Jihad in the Cause of God," Qutb lent his scholarly endorsement to the slogan coined by Hassan al-Banna, his immediate forerunner in the Muslim Brotherhood, "Prepare for Jihad and become lovers of death." Eliot's poem ends, obscurely, with an invocation of peace from the Upanishads ("Shantih shantih shantih"); *Milestones* is a declaration of holy warfare. Its first major fruit was the student movement that brought the Ayatollah Khomeini to power in Iran in 1979, and Qutb's ghost hovers all too perceptibly over September 11 and the Madrid, London, and Sharm al-Sheikh bombings. If you search the Web site of the Iqra bookshop in Leeds (www.iqraleeds.org.uk), where Sidique Khan met with his little flock of adherents, you'll find a glowing tribute to Qutb in the section devoted to "Personalities." He and Malcolm X are the only modern Muslims to be so honored.

The Iqra (Arabic for "read") bookshop, said to be squashed between a kebab place and an electrician's, is probably a relatively innocent part of the London story, but it's interesting that, as in Conrad, bookshops always figure in the lives of revolutionaries, for we're dealing with people who are, or were, intellectuals of a sort: students, or sometime students, with big transforming ideas on their minds. To call them "religious fanatics," "evil," "mad" is a natural consoling reflex, but it evades the fact that they are much more familiar figures than we would like them to be, these secret sharers who were devotees of cricket, football, bodybuilding; caring teachers, fathers, husbands; who looked as if they were having the time of their lives when they went whitewater rafting in Bala only last month. What distinguishes them is that they fell in thrall, as students will, to an intoxicating idea that seemed to explain the world—an idea that has evolved a long way since Qutb's *Milestones* but which has its roots in that forty-year-old classic of radical Islamism.

It's harder now than it was a few years ago to get into the Islamist mind-set because so many Web sites (like that of al-Muhajiroun) have either been removed from the Net or gone into some cyber underground where inquisitive outsiders can't reach them. Some remain, like Hizb ut-Tahrir (www.hizb-ut-tahrir.org) and, to my mind, the most informative of all, *Nida'ul Islam* (www.islam.org.au), a magazine published in Lakemba, a Sydney suburb that appears, from all I can find out about it, to be much like Australia's answer to Streatham Hill. *Nida'ul Islam* bills itself as "an intellectual magazine," and so it is: to judge by its writing, it's the work of fluent (probably Australian-born) graduate students who are on at least as easy terms with Western literature and politics as they are with Arabic Koranic scholars. It has featured long interviews with revolutionary heroes (including Osama bin Laden), along with dense situational analyses of the hot spots of the Islamic world, from North Africa around the globe to the Philippines. Browsing through its back issues is an eerie experience because its language, though utterly familiar for the most part, has never been seen in the same publication, let alone on the same page or in the same sentence. Its tirades on the moral degeneracy of the West are part of the banal stock-in-trade of our own far right, while its (sometimes quite astute) assaults on Western imperialism might come straight from the mouths of our own far left. It's as if articles from *The Salisbury Review* and the *Socialist Worker* had got inextricably mixed up at the printer. The religious content—references to the Koran and the *hadith* (sayings of the Prophet), to *shirk* (idolatry), *kufr* (unbelief), *deen* (religion, or way of life), *ummah* (community of believers), *haram* (unlawful)—seems more like the obligatory spicing of the dish than the dish itself, which is a philosophy of revolution, at once Marxist and ultrareactionary.

Yet it is not incoherent. Its two-pronged hatred of the West, from right and left, is dangerously lucid, and it's not hard to imagine disaffected young men hugging this rhetoric to themselves as if it contained the revelatory secret to the perplexing mystery of the world they live in. Add God to the mixture, a sense of divine approbation, and one can see the seductive power of what *Nida'ul Islam* calls "the jihad strain." One can also guess at the total bewilderment of most of those young men's elders if they were to read the magazine, whose superior, jargon-scattered, insiderish political tone is impossibly remote from the ordinary practice of Islam, if only because it smacks so off-puttingly of the more questionable benefits of Western higher education.

One consistent theme in all the attacks launched by Islamist revolutionaries is that they have freely availed themselves of Western materials to use against the West. The September 11 hijackers turned Seattle-built Boeing jetliners into weapons of mass destruction. The London bombers used TATP (nicknamed "Mother of Satan") as their explosive—apparently one can buy all its necessary ingredients, like drain cleaner and hair bleach, at Tesco, though you'd probably need a bachelor of science in chemistry to successfully assemble it. The same principle applies to their ideas: most are off-the-shelf items from the Western intellectual hypermarket, from their adaptation of the patrician high modernist line on the decadence of the West to their Frantz Fanon–like advocacy of violence as the answer to colonial oppression.

Such ideas alone would lead to nothing much more than groups of students sitting about glumly in cafés, agreeing on the injustice and rottenness of the world, and of course the detonator is a feverish and self-aggrandizing kind of religious belief, a raging thirst for martyrdom. A fellow passenger described how one of the July 21 would-be bombers carefully laid his body over his rucksack in order to embrace the blast that would transport him to eternity. That shocking movement, at least, doesn't come out of the West but out of the dark and twisted extremities of Salafism and its glamorization of death in jihad. (I'm assuming here, despite some rumors to the contrary, that the July 7 bombers were bent on suicide and not "mules," duped into staying with their bombs for ten minutes too long.)

It's this explosive combination of potent, essentially Western ideas and fervent supernatural belief, the *Milestones* formula, which we now confront—not an exotic alien import but a hybrid that can spring up almost anywhere in the tackier quarters of our own cities, whose whole character lies in their mongrel, disorderly heterogeneity, and where everything and everybody tend to get mixed up with everything and everybody else. To the student revolutionist, his home streets are living symbols of the Western decadence he has learned to despise, clear evidence of the truth of the message delivered to him via book, imam, or Internet. Here—let's call it Streatham Hill—is all the impurity and corruption, the new *jahiliyyah*, of the degenerate West.

And so it is with the issue of Iraq. Tony Blair is surely right on technical, and somewhat Clintonian, grounds when he insists that British involvement in the US-led occupation is not the "cause" of the London bombings. What Iraq has supplied, to a Qutbist movement that long predates September 2001, is a whopping pretext. Every photograph from Abu Ghraib, every story coming out of Bagram and Guantánamo Bay, every video of children killed in the early stages of the invasion or wedding party under aerial bombardment, gives further flesh to the idea of the West as a brutal imperial oppressor.

That these basic ideas, at least in their nonviolent form, are relatively wide-rooted in the British Muslim community at large was illustrated by a YouGov poll commissioned by *The Daily Telegraph* and published there on July 23. Although 77 percent of Muslims questioned thought the July 7 bombings were "not justified at all," 6 percent thought they were "on balance justified." To the question "Do you personally have any sympathy with the feelings and motives of those who carried out the bombings?," 13 percent answered, "Yes, a lot," and 11 percent said, "Yes, a little. Thirty-one percent agreed with the statement "Western society is decadent and immoral, and Muslims should seek to bring it to an end, but only by non-violent means." Although violence as the answer to Western decadence is overwhelmingly rejected (just 1 percent was for it), the broad terms of the Qutbist argument seem to be approved by nearly a third of all Muslims questioned—a much bigger slice than most of us might have expected.

Critical to the self-identity of the terrorist, however good or bad his cause, is the conviction that he's engaged in a just war. In *Under Western Eyes*, Haldin the assassin (and Conrad makes us believe that his motives are to be admired) says, "Don't make a mistake, Razumov. This is not murder—it is war, war." Repugnant as it may now seem to us, one can hear Sidique Khan saying exactly the same thing. To the jihadis, Iraq has lent a degree of plausibility, largely absent before the invasion, to their concept of just warfare.

At the end of the speech in which he exempts himself from murder, Haldin marvels sadly over how he became a reluctant assassin, driven to the "weary work" of killing:

> The Russian soul that lives in all of us...has a mission, I tell you, or else why should I have been moved to do this—reckless —like a butcher—in the middle of all these innocent people — scattering death—I! I!...I wouldn't hurt a fly!

That, too, from all we know about him, might have been said by Khan, the supposed ringleader and "recruiter" of the July 7 gang. One must take seriously the extraordinary testimonial to him, issued after the bombings by Sarah Balfour, the head teacher of Hillside Primary School in Beeston, where Khan had worked as a "learning mentor":

> He was great with the children and they all loved him. He did so much for them, helping and supporting them and running extra clubs and activities. Sidique was a real asset to the school and always showed 100% commitment.

The Khan remembered by Balfour would not have hurt a fly (as so many friends and relatives have said of both the September 11 hijackers and the London bombers). Like Haldin, he appears to have been driven to out-of-character butchery by an ungovernable idea that somehow lodged itself in his otherwise sound heart.

Last week, Tony Blair made an admirable statement: "We are not going to deal with this problem, with the roots as deep as they are, until we confront these people at every single level—and not just their methods but their ideas." It is a great step forward to acknowledge that the jihadis have ideas, an intellectual framework for their bloody missions, and are not motivated, as the Bush administration stubbornly continues to insist, by a spirit of pure evil-for-evil's-sake. Arguing with people's supernatural delusions is a losing game. But ideas are different. Ideas are negotiable: one can expose their false premises, concede their partial truth, disentangle their conclusions, rob them of their magic by the force of sweet reason. From what we know of the life stories of some of the London bombers, as of Ziad Jarrah, the September 11 hijacker, there's enough evidence to suggest that they would have been grateful, in a Haldin-like way, to have been liberated from the ideas that fatally infected them. With these particular ideas, we ought to be reasonably deft at helping to unravel them, since so many of them are—or were, in their original untwisted form —our own.

—July 2005

17

Coda

THE HAND

WAKING FROM AN UNPLEASANT dream before 5 AM, not by first light finding a crack in the drapes, for it's fifteen minutes or so too early for that, the roused sleeper's hand moves on an instinctive tour of the bedside table. This is familiar terrain, even in thick darkness: the easily upsettable plastic bottles of pills—aspirin, Diazepam, B-blockers, C-blockers, melatonin. The experienced hand knows every one, and slides stealthily between them. It weaves its way around the half-empty tumbler of grapefruit juice, and over the face-down paperback copy of *The Last Chronicle of Barset* until it reaches what it was searching for: the knurled volume knob of the elderly, tinny transistor radio whose broken antenna was long ago replaced with a wire coat hanger.

It seems to be the hand more than the sleeper himself that is so anxious for news as it switches on the radio and warily retreats back inside the covers. At 4:55, the local NPR station is still tuned to the BBC World Service, and there's a sports roundup on: cricket scores from a test match, something about the UEFA Cup; not what the hand was trying to find. When the station goes over at 5 to NPR's *Morning Edition* and the first news of the day from Washington, D. C., the sleeper jerks into full wakefulness in time for the lead headline.

This is how mornings begin nowadays, with the vague, routine apprehension of atrocity that almost never happens, but happens just frequently enough to justify the hand's habitual excursion across the bedside table. Pacific Standard Time is partly to blame, for the worst things in the world tend to take place while the West Coast is sleeping, or meant to be asleep. Baghdad, Cairo, Rome, Madrid, London, have survived the conventional hours of atrocity by 5 AM PST; New York is just about to enter them.

More IEDs in Iraq...more marines killed.... The hand embarks on its return journey to the radio and the sleeper goes back to the difficult business of sleeping. No atrocity—at least none of the anticipated kind—today, so far. Hours later, diddling away at his computer, he'll click on the BBC Web site at unreasonably frequent intervals, to make sure that *it* (and he has a very indistinct notion of what *it* is) hasn't yet taken place. In daylight, he'll jeer at this behavior as both symptomatic of a neurosis he needs to take in hand and a feckless excuse for goofing-off from work. But he still does it, nonetheless, and dates these unhealthy habits back to September 11, 2001—four years' worth of broken sleep and lost threads in his professional life.

Fear is the smallest ingredient of this compulsion, morbid enthrallment a much bigger one. On the morning, and through much of the afternoon, of July 7, 2005, I was glued to the TV in a house in south London, nearly six miles and a million or so people from the nearest of the explosions. Real shock was an unavailable emotion, so long had an attack on London been a "not if but when" eventuality: the best I could manage was surprise that it had happened on this day and at that hour. There were of course shocking details, but they were familiar, of the kind one glimpses involuntarily when being waved past the scene of a major car crash. Pity for the victims? Yes, but insufficient pity, too overlaid by less worthy feelings—the sense of being sucked into the city-stopping drama of the event, the unfolding *whodunit* and *whydunit*, the rating of hurriedly called press conference performances at the G8 summit up in Gleneagles (Blair good, Bush astonishingly inept), and, overwhelmingly, the certainty that this was not, or not quite, *it*. With no collapsing towers, no panicked crowds racing through smoke-filled streets, no five-figure estimates of likely casualties, the London bombings, though every bit as devastating to those involved as to the victims and families of September 11, looked, to the heartless eye of the TV viewer, like global terrorism slightly lite.

There's a certain perverse appetite that prompts the waking before dawn and the groping hand as it feels its way to the radio in the dark. As we get increasingly caught up in asymmetric warfare, one of whose central definitions is that it blurs the distinction between "military" and "civilian" to the point of nonexistence, we may perhaps be beginning to acquire some of that dangerous thirst for adrenalin that keeps soldiers being soldiers. A friend's brother—an American lieutenant colonel in the reserves, just back from a year's stint in Iraq—reports that some of the jolliest moments in the Green Zone occurred when the American embassy came under attack from volleys of rocket-propelled grenades. Office staff and soldiers would be sent sprawling from one side of a corridor to the other, everyone turning white with falling debris from Saddam's palatial baroque stucco ceilings, and frosted with bits of glass from Saddam's shattered chandeliers. Then would come the inevitable remark, spoken in a tone of enormous satisfaction, "That was a big one!"

Big ones—when you survive them—feed the addiction that makes war tolerable, and, more than that, enjoyable, for the warriors. They keep the necessary flow of adrenalin running through the veins. So, as the disembodied hand snakes past the pill bottles, themselves a piquant memento mori, some truant synapse in the brain anticipates the rush that only the baddest of bad news can bring. It is, one might say, just one more of those post–September 11 things, this insidious and corrupting mental adjustment to the events of the last four years, this disconnect between mind and motor response, this guilty, secret hunger for catastrophe.

—August 2005